A Season in the CONGO

A Season
in the CONGO

a play by Aimé Césaire

translated by Ralph Manheim

Grove Press, Inc., New York

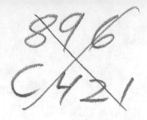

A Season in the CONGO

Characters

The Salesman (Lumumba)

Mokutu

Mama Makosi

Basilio

General Massens

Kala Lubu

Mpolo

Hammarskjöld

Croulard

Isaac Kalonji

Hélène

Pauline Lumumba

Okito

Tzumbi

Travélé

Msiri

Matthew Cordelier

The Sanza Player

Two Belgian policemen

The Voice

A Man

First Woman

Second Woman

Two Jailers

The Warden

Five Bankers

A Bakongo Tribesman

Four Radio Voices

Zimbwé

Three Senators

Ambassador of the Grand
    Occident

Voice of Civil War

Three Ministers

The Bishop

A Pilot

Ghana

A Mercenary

Onlookers

Soldiers

A group of girls

ACT 1

Scene 1

African quarter of Leopoldville . . . Natives are gathered around a SALESMAN *who is making a speech. Beer is being dispensed from a stand. Two* BELGIAN COPS *are looking on rather suspiciously.*

SALESMAN: Friends, the white men have invented a lot of things and brought them here to our country, good things and bad things. I won't stop to talk about the bad things today. But take it from me, friends, one of the good things is beer. My advice to you is to drink. Drink and drink some more. Come to think of it, do they leave us free to do anything else? If we get together, we end in jail. Hold a meeting? Jail. Write an article? Jail. Try to leave the country? Jail. And more of the same. But you don't have to take my word for it. Use your own eyes. I've been talking to you now for a good fifteen minutes, and their cops don't interfere . . . I've been doing the country from Stanleyville to Katanga, and their cops haven't bothered me! Why? Because I'm selling beer. Yes, you could say that here

1

in the Congo a mug of beer is the symbol of all our rights and liberties.

But not so fast. Same as there are different races in one and the same country—that's right, even in Belgium they have their Flemings and their Walloons, and everybody knows there's nothing worse than the Flemish—there are different kinds of beer. Different races and families of beer. And I've come here to tell you about the best of the lot: Polar Beer.

Polar, the freshness of the poles in the heat of the tropics. Polar, the beer of Congolese freedom! Polar, the beer of Congolese friendship and brotherhood!

ONLOOKER: Sure! But I've heard that Polar makes a fellow impotent. Takes away your *ngolo*. What do you say to that?

SALESMAN: That's a mean crack, citizen. If I wanted to give you a mean answer, I'd tell you to lend me your wife or sister for a few minutes.

Laughter in the crowd.

ONLOOKER: Ho, ho! He's got what it takes.

SALESMAN: But why not ask those girls over there, those lovely little girls; we'll put it up to them. What about it, girls? You with the beaming smiles, you with the smooth snake bellies: you tell us what's what.

THE GIRLS (*singing*):

> Women smooth as mirrors
> Bodies without guile
> Honey fritters,
> Hair a shimmering water.
> Two ripe and flawless
> Papayas for breasts.

Applause in the crowd.

FIRST BELGIAN COP: Not bad, his spiel. He's got a tongue in his head.

SECOND BELGIAN COP: I suppose so. But it's got me worried. That beer mug of his is a grab bag. You never know what he's going to pull out of it next. I've got a mind to ask him a question or two.

FIRST BELGIAN COP: Watch your step. We can't interfere with the sales of Polar Beer. Don't you know who owns Polar?

SECOND BELGIAN COP: How should I? All I know is that that nigger's dangerous.

FIRST BELGIAN COP: You're young. Just listen to me. The Minister's behind Polar . . . That's right . . . The Minister for the Congo! Knocks you for a loop, eh? But that's how it is. So now you see what's what. Come on, let's have a glass.

SECOND COP: Suits me. But let's take that salesman's name . . . Something tells me we're going to need it.

FIRST COP: Don't worry. We've got it. It's on file. His name is Patrice Lumumba.

SECOND BELGIAN COP: And what about him over there? Is he on file too?

FIRST BELGIAN COP: Oh, he's only a sanza player. Harmless. But a nuisance. He's everywhere all at once. Like a fly. And always buzzing.

SANZA PLAYER (*sings*):

> *Ata-ndele* . . . [Sooner or later . . .]

Scene 2

Waiters and customers moving about. They are setting up an African bar. Meanwhile a voice rises off-stage, growing louder and louder.

THE VOICE: Hear, hear! The buffalo is wounded. Plugged full of bullets, he's at the end of his strength. He's gone mad. Who's the buffalo? The buffalo is the Belgian government. And now that the buffalo's wounded, he's threatening us right and left, What do you say? You going to let his threats get you down? The buffalo is a brute. Are you afraid of his brutality? Of his heavy tread? This is the song of our ancestors:

> The buffalo has a heavy tread,
> A heavy tread, a heavy tread.
> If you see him, don't be afraid of his heavy tread,
> His heavy tread, his heavy tread.

The bar has been set up. Glaring light. Small tables. Men and prostitutes are moving about.

FIRST WOMAN (*singing*):

> Come, don't be afraid.
> I'm not a married woman.
> I married too soon.
> I thought there was nobody else.
> Oh, if I'd only known!

(*Approaching a table full of men.*) Really, Congo people have no manners. Men drinking beer all by themselves while a poor girl dies of thirst.

A MAN (*whistles*): And what a girl! Say, boys, she's high octane. Move over, friends, there's plenty of room. Sit down, baby, sit down.

SECOND WOMAN (*approaching*): Hey, girls, help! Help! I've had an accident. I'm losing my *jikita*. Those Belgian waistbands are no good. Rotten cork, that's all they are. Damn Belgians, they cheat us every way they can.

A MAN: They cheat us, they exploit us; that's right, lady-o, they exploit us. Black people are just too trusting.

FIRST WOMAN (*stripping*): I've solved the problem. I've given up the *jikita*. The *jibula's* the dress for me.

MAN (*laughing*): More like undress. Take it easy, sister. The slightest move in that get-up unveils the thighs. And plenty more. Hee, hee! Plenty more.

SECOND WOMAN: Is that any way to talk to a lady? It's free, isn't it, so why complain? Ah, men are getting stingy and mean. Anyway, I'm sick of it all. (*Singing.*)

> Listen, friends,
> God gave us mothers,
> Mothers who kill us for money,
> For money and more money.

Enter MOKUTU *in European dress. He looks like a pimp.*

MOKUTU: Boys and girls, howdy! I've got news for you. The Belgians have arrested Patrice, they wouldn't listen to reason. They've taken him to Elisabethville in handcuffs, and meanwhile the politicians are sitting around the table in Brussels, deciding the fate of the

Congo. If those African politicians had any guts, they'd boycott the conference until Patrice is released.

MAN: Well, that's one way of looking at it. But isn't the fate of the country more important than the fate of one man?

MOKUTU: Oh, oh! Have we got Belgians around here? Black Belgians? Tell me, friend, did you ever stop to think that the fate of the country might depend on the fate of one man?

MAN: Okay, okay. But what are we going to do? Do you want us to storm the Elisabethville prison with our bare hands?

MOKUTU: Christ, how do I know? Just do something. Anything you can do in the Congo today is a step toward the revolution. Do what you like. As long as you do something.

SANZA PLAYER (*his voice rises off-stage and sings the hymn of the Kibanguists*):

> We are the orphan children,
> Dark is the night, hard is the way.
> Almighty God, who's going to help us?
> Father Congo, who's going to give us a hand?

FIRST WOMAN: I suggest we go into mourning for six months. That's what you do when you lose a member of the family, and I call Patrice a member of the family.

MOKUTU: Don't make me laugh. Is that any skin off the Belgians' ass?

SECOND WOMAN: I say we go on strike and parade with our banners. All our organizations, the Lolita Club, the Dollar Association, the Free Woman, marching up and down with our flags—yellow, green, and red—that'll put their eye out.

MAMA MAKOSI [*the Mighty Madame*]: Baloney. No mourning, no strike. Work is work. We'll work. Harder than ever. We'll raise bail. The buffalo likes money. He feeds on money. And Patrice will sit at the table in Brussels with the rest of them. I have spoken.

MOKUTU: Friends, I've got to leave you now. Do what your hearts tell you. Anything you do for Patrice is good. Thank you.

SANZA PLAYER (*stands up and sings; the song is taken up by the crowd*):

> When the rainy season comes,
> War will come too,
> The season of red blood.
> The buffalo's strong and the elephant's strong.
> Where can we hide?
> Their science doesn't tell us.
> The buffalo will fall,
> The elephant will fall,
> They'll feel the heavy hand of God.
> The blood-red season's coming.
> The season of our freedom.

Scene 3

Elisabethville prison.

FIRST JAILER (*on the phone*): Hello, yes, sir . . . Certainly, sir . . .

SECOND JAILER: What is it, boss? Bad news?

FIRST JAILER: It's the warden. He's on his way over. Something about Mister Patrice Lumumba.

SECOND JAILER: What a pest he turned out to be! I've seen a lot of prisoners in my time, but take it from me, there's nothing worse than an eggheaded nigger.

FIRST JAILER: You can say that again. Who does he think he is? He's even started writing poetry. Since when do baboons write poetry? All right, bring him in, we'll get him into shape to see the warden.

While the SECOND JAILER *goes out and returns with* LU-MUMBA, *the* FIRST JAILER *reads.*

Get a load of this!

> "Congo, and then the white men came
> Raping your women and making
> Your warriors drunk.
> But the future will bring deliverance.
> The banks of the great river will be yours,

8

Yours this land and all its riches,
Yours the sun in the sky."

Where does he get that stuff about the sun? I knew
they wanted our houses and our women. Now they even
want our sun . . . Oh, so there you are, you bastard.
Ungrateful dog! So His Nibs writes poetry. Just tell me
this, you baboon, who taught you how to read?
Couldn't have been the no-good Belgians, could it? All
right, I'm going to give you a little poetry in the ribs.
(*He hits* LUMUMBA.)

SECOND JAILER: You don't know the half of it. Look what
I found in his cell. The manuscript of an article pro-
testing against his imprisonment. Claims it's illegal—
that's what they all say. Demands to be set free so he
can attend the Round Table conference in Brussels.
Signed: Patrice Lumumba, president of the NCM.

FIRST JAILER: That's rich. (*He hits* LUMUMBA *again.*) So
His Blackness wants to go to Brussels, eh? And what
would you say to the king if you saw him? What would
you say to the Bwana Kitoko?

SECOND JAILER (*hitting* LUMUMBA): I guess he wants to be
a minister! (*He laughs.*) His Excellency, the baboon! . . . His Excellency.

FIRST JAILER: Maybe so. But he'll have to eat King Kala
first. Easy there, son. Don't rough him up too much.
The warden'll be here any minute. Hm. Here he
comes.

Enter THE WARDEN.

THE WARDEN: Mr. Lumumba, I bring you good news. Yes,
believe it or not, occasionally a warden has good news
for a prisoner: I've just received word from Brussels.
His Excellency the Minister for the Congo has decided

to release you. He wishes you, as president of the NCM —the National Congo Movement, as you call it—to attend the Round Table conference. I have been instructed to do everything in my power to help you prepare for the trip. There's a Sabena plane for Brussels tomorrow. You are free, Mr. Lumumba. Bon voyage, Your Excellency!

THE JAILERS: Good grief! (*They bow.*) Bon voyage, Your Excellency!

The SANZA PLAYER *passes, singing:*

> *Kongo Mpaka Dima* [Be watchful, brothers, the Congo is moving.]

Scene 4

A sign is lowered from the grid, saying: Brussels, Confer-
ence Room. The antechamber of a room in the palace. Four
or five men, caricatures of bankers—dinner jacket, top hat,
big cigar—are pacing about. Indignation and panic; they
have just heard through indiscretion that at Lumumba's re-
quest the Belgian government has set the date for Congolese
independence at June 30, 1960.

FIRST BANKER: We're screwed. A government of traitors
   has given away our empire.

SECOND BANKER: They've set the date for independence.

THIRD BANKER: They've knuckled under to that baboon.

FIFTH BANKER: Chin up, gentlemen. Chin up, I say. You've
   got to wed the spirit of the times. I don't say love her,
   it's enough to wed her. There's nothing so frightening
   about this independence.

FIRST BANKER:
   What's this? You shrug your shoulders at a blow
   That will disrupt the state and dam the flow
   Of our finances. Good Lord, this will make
   Belgium a third-rate power, a Liechtenstein!

FOURTH BANKER:
   Your attitude is dangerous. Do you mean
   It, or is that a sample of your wit?

11

I'm a plain man, and I'll speak straight
From the shoulder. When ruin threatens a great state,
It's not the time for liberal ideas.

FIFTH BANKER:

My friend, when ruin threatens a great state,
The only good ideas are bold ideas.

FIRST BANKER:

We've heard enough of your obscurities.
Come to the point. If you have got some plan,
Let's hear it. Speak up. Make some suggestion, man.
Don't stand there looking wise.

SECOND BANKER:

That's telling him. Have you a policy?

FIFTH BANKER:

Policy? Hm. That's maybe too much said,
But some ideas have shaped up in my head.
No credit due. It's normal after twenty
Years in the tropics, time to find out plenty.
To handle savages, there are two ways:
One is the club, but that's seen better days.
The other is the purse.

FIRST BANKER:

Go on.

FIFTH BANKER:

All right, I'll spell it out. Just pay attention.
What do their leaders want? They want to be
Presidents, ministers, living in luxury.
In short, the purse! High-powered cars,
Villas, high wages, cushy bank accounts.
Spare no expense. Just grease their palms and stuff
Them. The investment will pay off.
You'll see, their hearts will melt. And presently
Those smirking, smiling politicians will be

A special class between us and their people.
They'll hold the people down provided we
Tie them with bonds—well, maybe not of friendship,
That's out of date in this sad century—
But knots and tangles of complicity.

FIRST BANKER: Bravo! Good man! We're with you.

CHORUS OF BANKERS: Hurrah! Hurrah! Three cheers for independence.

Scene 5

*Leopoldville. The crowd is celebrating independence. At-
mosphere of friendly good nature. The "Independence Hot-
cha-cha" is heard.*

A WOMAN: How's Dependa going to get here? By car? By
boat? Or by airplane?

FIRST MAN: She's coming with the little white king, Bwana
Kitoko. He's bringing her.

SANZA PLAYER: Listen to me, citizens. Nobody's bringing us
Dependa. We're taking her.

THE BAKONGO TRIBESMAN: It's all the same. Maybe they're
giving us Dependa and maybe we're taking her, but
one thing is sure: Now that we've got her, we're going
to send all those Bengalas back to their villages. The
Bengalas are wrecking the country.

FIRST MAN: Watch your step, sir. Don't try to provoke us.
If you ask me, it's pretty nice of us to put up with a
Bakongo president, to let a Bakongo rule us. By rights
a river man should have the job. Jean Bolikango!
That's the man! Hurrah for Jean Bolikango!

MPOLO: That's enough, gentlemen. Calm down. Let's not
have tribal quarrels. That's just what the colonialists
want. Divide and rule, that's their motto. We've got

14

to stop being Bengalas, Bakongos, and Batetelas. From now on we're all just plain Congolese, free, united, and organized. Let's all drink a good glass of beer to our unity. Be my guests, gentlemen.

FIRST MAN: Good idea. But the question is: what kind of beer? I only drink Polar.

SECOND MAN: Primus is my brand.

THIRD MAN: Primus, the queen of beers. That's King Kala's brand.

FIRST MAN: It's Polar for me: the freshness of the poles in the heat of the tropics.

MPOLO: Let's drink to peace. To every kind of peace, peace in our hearts, peace between tribes, peace between the different brands of beer. Drink, gentlemen, Polar or Primus, it's all the same. So long as we drink to the Congo!

ALL: Here's to the Congo! (*They sing the "Independence Hot-cha-cha."*)

Scene 6

Somewhere in Leopoldville. BASILIO, *King of Belgium, and* GENERAL MASSENS, *Commander of the Congolese militia, standing before the curtain.*

BASILIO: Not so long ago this barbarous people lay stunned beneath the heavy fist of Stanley, of Boula Matari, the Rock Crusher, as they call him out here. We took them in hand. Yes, Providence entrusted them to our care, we fed them, cared for them, educated them. The independence I am granting them today will show whether we have succeeded in bettering their nature, whether our efforts have been rewarded. Freedom will put them to the test. Either they will set all Africa an example, as we ourselves have done in Europe: the example of a united, self-respecting, hard-working people. In that case the emancipation of our wards will redound to the eternal glory of Belgium. Or else the barbaric root, nurtured in the moldering depths, will regain its noxious vigor and stifle the good seed sown for the last fifty years by the untiring devotion of our missionaries. In that case . . .

GENERAL MASSENS: In that case?

BASILIO: We'll see about that when the time comes, Massens. Meanwhile, let's put our trust in human nature.

GENERAL MASSENS: Your Majesty, these experiments bear
witness to your generosity, your genius. But you know
how I feel about it. I have my doubts . . .

However, if such is your sovereign will, I have only
one recommendation. Make it clear to them that you
have given them this freedom—this hashish that in-
toxicates them with such deplorable visions—and that
they haven't conquered it. Perhaps they are not too
obtuse to grasp the big difference between a right they
have earned and the gift of your Royal Munificence.

BASILIO: Don't worry, Massens. I will make that very clear.
But here they are.

The curtain rises, disclosing LUMUMBA, KALA, *other
Congolese delegates, and, in the background, the Congolese crowd.*

KALA LUBU (*President of the Congolese Republic, to* LU-
MUMBA): Mr. Mayor, oh, I beg your pardon, Mr. Prime
Minister, I mean. The essential thing, in my opinion, is
that this ceremony should pass off smoothly, that we
observe the proprieties. The rules of good manners demand it, the rules of politics as well. This is no time for
complaints and recriminations, for high-sounding—or
low-sounding—words. Childbirth is never painless;
that's the law of nature. But when the child is born,
everyone smiles. Today I want to see a Congo wreathed
in smiles. But here's the King. (*Addressing the crowd.*)
All together now, Long live the King!

THE CROWD: Long live the King! Hurrah for Bwana Kitoko! Hurrah for King Kala!

The crowd waves little flags with the sign of the kodi,
*a shell pierced with a sword, emblem of the Abako,
Kala's political organization. Firecrackers are set off.
A group of black children led by a bearded mission-*

ary sing a song in the style of the Vienna Sängerkna-
ben.

BASILIO: I shall be brief. A word in pious recollection of
my predecessors who were the guardians of this country
before me, and first of all of Leopold, the founder,
who came here not to take, not to dominate, but to
give and to bring civilization. And a word of gratitude
to all those who built up this country day by day—
at the cost of untold hardships. Glory to the founders!
And glory to those who carried on their work. And
now, gentlemen, I give you this State, the work of our
hands. We are a nation of engineers and manufac-
turers. I can say without boasting that we are putting
an excellent machine into your hands; take good care
of it, that's all I ask of you. But since it is a machine,
mechanical difficulties can reasonably be foreseen, and
it goes without saying that you can come to us with
your problems, that you can count on our assistance;
our disinterested assistance, gentlemen. And now, men
of the Congo, take over the controls, the eyes of the
whole world are upon you!

KALA LUBU: Sire! Your august Majesty's presence at the
ceremonies of this memorable day is new and striking
proof of your solicitude for this people that you have
loved and protected. The people of the Congo have
received your message of friendship with respect and
fervent devotion. They will long bear in their hearts
the words you have just addressed to them in this
solemn hour. They will never cease to prize the friendship which the Belgian government has offered them
and will unstintingly do their part to maintain a sincere collaboration between our two nations. People of
the Congo, my brothers, I want you to know, to understand, that independence has not come to our country
to abrogate law or tribal custom; it has come to com-

plete them, to fulfill and harmonize them. Nor has independence come to us to undo the work of civilization.
Independence comes to us under the twofold guidance
of Custom and Civilization. Independence has come to
reconcile the old and the new, the nation and its tribes.
If we keep faith with Civilization and with Custom,
God will protect the Congo.

Uncertain applause.

LUMUMBA: As for me, Sire, my thoughts are for those who
have been forgotten. We are the people who have been
dispossessed, beaten, mutilated; the people whom the
conquerors treated as inferiors, in whose faces they
spat. A people of kitchen boys, house boys, laundry
boys, in short, a people of boys, of yes-bwanas, and
anyone who wanted to prove that a man is not neces-
sarily a man could take us as an example.
Sire, whatever suffering, whatever humiliation could
be known, we have known it.
But comrades, they were not able to dull our taste
for life, and we resisted.
We didn't have much to fight with, but we fought,
we fought for fifty years.
And today we have won.
Today our country is in the hands of its children.
This sky, this river, these lands are ours.
Ours the lake and the forest,
Ours Karissimbi, Nyiragongo, Niamuragira, Mikeno,
Ehu, mountains sprung from the word of fire.
People of the Congo, this is a great day.
It is the day when the nations of the world welcome
Congo our mother,
and still more Congo our child,
child of our sleepless nights, of our sufferings, of our
struggles.
Comrades and brothers in combat, it is up to us to

transform each of our wounds into a nurturing
   breast,
each of our thoughts, our hopes, into a fountain of
   change.
Kongo! Watch me. I raise him above my head;
I put him back on my shoulder;
Three times I spit in his face;
I set him down on the ground, and I ask you; tell me
   the truth, do you know this child? And you all
   answer: it's Kongo, our king.
I wish I were a toucan, that wonderful bird, to cross the
   skies announcing to races and tongues that Kongo
   has been born to us, our king. Long live Kongo!
Kongo, late born, may he follow the sparrow hawk!
Kongo, late born, let him have the last word!
Comrades, everything remains to be done, or done over,
   but we will do it, we will do it over. For Kongo.
We will remake all the laws, one by one, for Kongo.
We will revise all the customs, one by one, for Kongo.
Uprooting injustice, we will rebuild the old edifice
   piece by piece, from cellar to attic, for Kongo.
That which is bowed shall be raised, and that which is
   raised shall be raised higher—for Kongo!
   I demand the union of all.
I demand the devotion of every man. For Kongo!
   Uhuru! Freedom!

A moment of ecstasy.

Congo! These are great days!
When this day's rags and this day's tinsel have been
   burned,
Let us advance rejoicing to my unanimous step
Into the new day! Into the solstice!

Stupor. Enter the first four BANKERS.

FIRST BANKER: Terrible, terrible! It was bound to end this way.

SECOND BANKER: That speech! This time we're through. We can pack our bags.

THIRD BANKER (*with great dignity*): Obviously. Where order breaks down, the banker packs his bags.

FOURTH BANKER: Poor Congo, drifting on uncharted seas!

MOKUTU *passes. He is preoccupied and sees no one.*

MOKUTU: And I picked him for a winner. Who could have written that speech of his? And to think I thought I could make a statesman out of him! Well, if he wants to break his neck, it's his funeral. Too bad! Too bad! Knife oversharpened cuts its sheath. (*He spits.*)

SANZA PLAYER (*perplexed*): Let's not be too quick to judge the boss. He must have had his reasons even if we can't see them.

Enter LUMUMBA.

LUMUMBA: Well, did you like what I said? Or are you one of those people who think the sky is going to fall because a black man has the audacity to give a king a piece of his mind with the whole world listening in? No, you don't like it. I can see it in your eyes.

MOKUTU: Since you're asking me, let me tell you a little story.

LUMUMBA: I hate stories.

MOKUTU: Just to save time. When I was a boy, I went hunting with my grandfather. One day I found myself face to face with a leopard. I lost my head. I threw my javelin and wounded him. My grandfather was furious. He made me go in and retrieve the spear. That day I understood, once and for all, that you don't attack a beast unless you're sure of killing him.

LUMUMBA (*very coldly*): You're wrong if you're against what I said. There was a taboo that needed breaking. I broke it. As for your story, if it means that you hate the Beast—colonialism—and that you're determined to hunt it down to a finish with me . . . everything will be all right.

MOKUTU: Did you ever doubt it, Patrice?

LUMUMBA (*brusquely*): Good. That's enough for me. Let's make up.

They go out. The SANZA PLAYER *comes in and sings the Lupeto song.*

SANZA PLAYER:

> Nobody's better
> At sniffing the wind.
> They haven't the mugs
> Of murdering thugs,
> But noses to sniff out the wind.
> They're the lupeto boys.
>
> Those boys like to eat,
> They don't care where they get it
> As long as they can eat it.
> They're the lupeto boys.
>
> You ask me what's lupeto.
> You haven't understood.
> Lupeto's money, lucre, dough,
> They're neither bad nor good.
> They're the lupeto boys.

Enter the FIFTH BANKER.

FIRST BANKER:

    Congratulations for your shrewd advice!

FIFTH BANKER:

    Colleague and friend, I think you're being unfair.
    Risks are the price of politics, the price
    Of any action.

SECOND BANKER:

    Phrases, words, hot air.
    Your plan goes wrong, and you stand there and gas.

FIFTH BANKER:

    Phrases, why, not at all. Chin up, my friends!
    Shall we lie down like bathmats at the first
    Love tap? No, listen. Follow my idea. (*He whispers
    in their ears.*)
    If self-determination is the style,
    It can't be helped. But then, why not for all?
    For you and me, it's only logical.
    You catch my drift, you read between the lines?
    Then self-determination for our mines!

FIRST BANKER:

    Hush, hush! Let's listen, please.
    Our colleague often gets some good ideas.

FIFTH BANKER:

    Friends, when I see this turmoil, this commotion,
    I realize there's only one solution.
    Yes, when I see this Congo, this immense
    Chaotic mass, it simply doesn't make sense
    That our Katanga, our beloved nation,
    Shouldn't cast loose. That's self-determination.

FIRST BANKER:

    Ah, now you're talking, pal. I love you. Self-
    Determined uranium? That's the ticket, eh?

FIFTH BANKER:
> And not just uranium. Diamonds, copper, cobalt.
> All Katanga. Shining, clinking, gilt-edged Katanga.

CHORUS OF BANKERS: Hurrah! Hurrah! Three cheers for
Katanga!

Scene 7

A night club. A record is playing "Franco de Mi Amor."
When it stops, a woman's voice is heard over the radio.

FIRST VOICE: This is the voice of African Moral Rearmament. Get to work, citizens. To work! And when I say "to work," it's the same as if I were saying "to arms." We are at war, citizens, at war for the future of the Congo. The mobilization of the working classes must be total, unconditional, deliberate, voluntary. The Congo has been living in prehistoric times. With independence we have acceded to the historical age, and that means the age of hard work. To work, citizens! To work!

Another voice is heard.

SECOND VOICE: People of the Congo, wake up. Don't let yourselves be brainwashed! Come out of your holes, your workshops, your factories. Make yourselves heard, demand your rights. Independence, yes! But don't let it be an empty word. Take it from me, citizens, it's not empty for everybody. Ask the members of parliament, ask the ministers. Who gets the cars? Who gets the women? The ministers, the members of parliament! Who gets Santa Claus? The eggheads. We de-

25

mand Santa Claus for everybody! That's what we
mean by independence. Hurrah for independence!

The stage is invaded by Congolese SOLDIERS, *half
drunk, swinging their belts. They shout rhythmically:*

Down with the politicians! Down with Lumumba,
Lumumba *pamba*, Lumumba *pamba!* . . .

Scene 8

Leopoldville, the prime minister's office.

LUMUMBA: Get me Makessa. Where's Kangolo? Absent. Some office manager. No use looking for Sissoko. He's asleep. He never gets up in the daytime. Maybe you think things can go on like this? No, goddammit, they can't. Gentlemen, who are we? Well, I'm going to tell you who we are. We're slaves. I'm a slave, a voluntary slave. You're all slaves, or you ought to be, and by slaves I mean men condemned to work without rest. You have no right to rest. You're here to serve the Congo twenty-four hours a day. Private life is out. But at least you're free from material worries . . . because you won't have time for any. I know, I know. They say I ask too much, they say I'm adventurous, foolhardy and so on. Is that it? They say I'm trying to go too fast. Well, you no-good snails, let me tell you this. We've got to go fast, we've got to go too fast. Do you know how much time I have to catch up with fifty years of history? Three months, gentlemen. And you think I can afford to take it easy?

MPOLO: Mr. President, the soldiers! The soldiers are coming.

LUMUMBA: Soldiers? What in hell do they want? What are they squawking about?

27

MPOLO: They're yelling, "Kill Lumumba. Lumumba *pamba!*"

LUMUMBA (*flying into a rage*): Is that all? The bastards, the traitors. Belgians, that's what they are. Lousy Flemish bastards! When I think that for fifty years they crawled for the Belgians. And the minute we settle our African asses to give them an African government, they come around snapping at our ankles.

A MINISTER: Well, if you ask me, independence is getting off to a lovely start.

LUMUMBA: Idiot! How did you expect it to start? And how do you expect it to go on? What did you think? When I picked you as my ministers, did you think I was inviting you to a picnic? I won't try to fool you, gentlemen. There's going to be trouble, every kind of trouble before you can say Jack Sprat: mutiny, sabotage, threats, slander, blackmail, and treason. You look surprised. That's what power means: betrayal, maybe death. Yes, death and no maybe. That's the Congo. The Congo, you see, is a country where things go fast. A seed in the ground today, tomorrow a bush, no, tomorrow a forest. In any case, the things that move quickly will keep on moving quickly. Don't count on me to slow them down. Mpolo, let those loud-mouthed bastards in, I'll speak to them . . . I'll move them. I'll turn their hearts.

Enter the soldiers' delegation.

Come in, gentlemen. Ah, it's too bad you haven't brought your civilian friends, those union leaders, who've suddenly got so brave when it comes to holding the knife to our throats. For fifty years they've kept their mouths shut and trembled at the sight of a Belgian. And now they refuse to give a Congolese govern-

ment, a government of their brothers, the few months'
time it needs to get its bearings. As for you soldiers, I
won't beat about the bush. Your demands are legitimate. I understand them and I intend to meet them.
When you were the militia, your officers were Belgians;
now that you're the National Army, you want to be
commanded by Congolese. That's perfectly reasonable.
And if we hesitated a moment before Africanizing the
Army, it was because our good will was blocked by the
ill will and the prejudices of General Massens. That
shows you what to expect of the colonialists. They're
obstinate, gentlemen, and they're underhanded. But
we have dismissed Massens.

SOLDIERS: Down with Massens!

LUMUMBA: Massens is gone and the government will meet
your demands. Each one of you is being promoted to
the next higher rank: every private will be a corporal,
every corporal a sergeant ...

SOLDIERS: No! No! Colonels! Generals!

MOKUTU: Mr. Prime Minister, the troops demand the total
and immediate Africanization of the officers' corps.
The way things stand, there isn't a moment to lose.

LUMUMBA: The government is not unaware of the problem.
As of the present moment I am in a position to inform
you that the government is considering . . . no, that
the government has decided to appoint a Congolese
general and a Congolese colonel immediately. The general is Lundula, the colonel is our secretary of state
for youth problems, Mpolo, here present.

SOLDIERS: No! We don't want Mpolo. He's not a soldier,
he's a politician. We want Mokutu. To hell with Mpolo.
We want Mokutu. He was in the militia for seven
years. He's a soldier.

LUMUMBA: You want Mokutu? Good. I ratify your choice. It's true, Mokutu's a soldier. And Mokutu's my friend, my brother. I know that Mokutu will never betray me. Mpolo was appointed by the government. Well, I appoint Mokutu. That settles it. But the question isn't whether you're going to be officers or not, because you are officers right now. The question is what kind of officers you choose to be: parade officers? Bakshish officers? A new caste? The government wants you to be officers of the Congolese people, fired with the spirit of the Congolese people and determined to fight like tigers to safeguard our Congolese independence. What do you say?

SOLDIERS: Yes! Yes! Hurrah for Lumumba!

LUMUMBA: Congolese soldiers and officers, if the enemy attacks us, and that may be sooner than we think, it's up to you . . . I expect him to burn his claws like a hawk that tries to steal meat from the villagers' fire.

    Long live the Congolese Army. Long live the Congo!

SOLDIERS: Hurrah! Hurrah!

The SANZA PLAYER *enters and sings:*

> Pollen of fire
> Drunken springtime
> A little bird is flitting
> Forgetful of snares
> Forgetting the blowpipe.
> Birdbrain, says the trap.
> The bird has forgotten the trap,
> The trap remembers the bird.

Scene 9

In the darkness white refugees cross the stage, carrying what few belongings they have been able to save. Suddenly red lights illumine an immense map of the Congo. On a balcony in the half-darkness two shadows: BASILIO *and* MASSENS.

FIRST RADIO VOICE: Marigold calling Gardenia, Marigold calling Gardenia. Answer, Gardenia.

SECOND RADIO VOICE: Betty calling Angela. Two cars full of women and children are headed for Kitona base. You will send troops to meet them.

THIRD RADIO VOICE: Marigold calling Gardenia. Latest news from Luluabourg, Kasai province. Twelve hundred Europeans barricaded in Immokasai building besieged by Congolese troops armed with mortars and machine guns. Send troops immediately. Urgent. Out.

FOURTH RADIO VOICE: Phoenix, do you read me, Phoenix? Dispatch received from Juba. Watsa troops in revolt. Forty Belgian officers with their families taken prisoner. They are being tortured. Urge immediate action. Out.

Enter BASILIO *and* MASSENS *in uniform.*

MASSENS: Well, your Majesty. Now we know. They've wrecked our Congo.

BASILIO: Alas!

MASSENS: Majesty, they're savages. Order must be restored, and I see only one way.

BASILIO: I know, Massens. But unfortunately international law doesn't allow it.

MASSENS: Your Majesty, this is no time to tie our hands with juridical scruples. Human lives are at stake, European lives. That's more important than any law.

BASILIO: You're right, Massens. That's more important than any law. Very well. I give you carte blanche.

MASSENS (*in a thundering voice*): Forward march!

A vision of Belgian paratroopers in action. Darkness.

LUMUMBA'S VOICE (*shouting the Congolese war cry*): People of the Congo! Luma! Luma!

The war tomtoms sound in the night, spreading the news of the Belgian attack.

Scene 10

LUMUMBA, KALA, *and a* PILOT *in a plane over Elisabethville. Wind, rain, lightning.*

LUMUMBA: Damn weather! Look! Look! The wind's uprooting the trees. And the rain! The weather's as bad as the situation in the Congo, and that's something. Looks like a herd of phantom elephants stampeding through a bamboo forest. Isn't it a little early for the rainy season to be starting?

KALA: Yes, the weather's bad. Definitely. . . But when God is perplexed, we ignorant mortals call it fog.

LUMUMBA: Pilot, aren't we going to land soon? This trip is interminable. Where are we?

PILOT: We'll be over Elisabethville in a moment. Have patience, your Excellency. We're in the middle of a tropical hurricane. Wait. The radio operator's trying to tell me something. (*A paper is handed him. He reads it aloud.*) Isn't that nice! Msiri and Tzumbi in person in the control tower. The Katanga authorities won't let us land.

LUMUMBA: Msiri? Tzumbi? The Katanga authorities? Are we or are we not the Congo authorities? Does Katanga belong to the Congo, or doesn't it? Pilot, I order you to land. Immediately.

PILOT: It can't be done, sir. Not in this weather. They've turned out the lights on the airstrip. Look, you can see for yourself.

LUMUMBA: Traitor! Flemish dog! You disobey me? Are you in cahoots with the secessionists?

As the plane regains altitude.

PILOT: Where do we head for, Mr. President?

KALA: Leopoldville.

LUMUMBA: No. It's arms that we need! Arms! To Moscow! To Moscow!

Scene 11

At the Congolese parliament in Leopoldville. As the SENA-
TORS *take their places, the* SANZA PLAYER *passes, singing*:

> Palm wine man climbing the palm tree,
> Come down, little ant,
> Come down, little sparrow,
> The good souls sing at the foot of the palm tree.
> Up you go, palm wine man, up you go,
> Sparrow drunk with freedom.

FIRST SENATOR: Honorable colleagues: The Congo has become a vast cemetery; the Belgians have been conduct-
ing themselves like the Roman legions.

SECOND SENATOR: I wish to call the attention of the government to our finances—yes, our finances. The Congolese
treasury has evaporated, the north wind has blown
it away. Where are we going to find money now? The
Bank of the Congo has been transferred to Katanga.
Are we going to sleep while Rome burns? That is the
question I ask the government. I for my part intend
to die in the toga of a senator.

THIRD SENATOR: Fellow senators! We haven't come here to
discourage each other. But there are some things that
cannot be passed over in silence. Our prime minister
and our president are never here. We must have the

35

courage to look the facts in the face. When we think
they are in Leo, they are in Matadi; when they are
supposed to be in Matadi, they are in Banana; in
Banana the word is that they've gone off to Moanda
or Boma. They fly right and left, all over the place,
and always the two of them. Gentlemen, it's customary
in a civilized country that when the husband goes out
the wife stays home.

LUMUMBA: I for my part, gentlemen, assure you that we
don't travel enough. Ah, I wish I could multiply and
divide myself, so as to be everywhere at once. In
Matadi, in Boma, in Elisabethville, in Luluabourg,
to crush the enemy's many-headed plot. For the plot
is everywhere. Ever since the very first day of our independence, I've seen the Belgians, men ravaged by
hatred and eaten by resentment, hatching their plot.
General Massens stirring up the militia against the
government, representing us as a gang of politicians
and unscrupulous profiteers. The Belgian ambassador,
Mynher Van den Putt, doing everything in his power
to sabotage, to undermine, to disorganize our republic,
putting pressure on all Belgian technicians and civil
servants to leave the country. From the very first day
General Massens has been setting the scene for his
raids, working up a pretext for his mercenaries to step
in. That's the Belgian plot, gentlemen. Their treaty
of friendship with us? As far as they are concerned,
it's a scrap of paper. We let them maintain staging
areas on our territory. They turn them into armed
camps from which to attack us. That's the Belgian
plot. They've shelled Kabalo, Boma, and Matadi! But
the worst was yet to come. Today, July 11, 1960,
Tzumbi, our brother Abraham Tzumbi, seconded by
Msiri, incited, advised, and financed by the Belgians,
has proclaimed the independence of Katanga, our
richest province, without consulting the population.

And what is the first act of this independent state?
To conclude a treaty of military assistance and eco-
nomic cooperation with Belgium. That's the Belgian
plot. Have I made myself clear? People of the Congo,
we've got to smash that plot. People of the Congo,
we have paid dearly for our independence. Are we
going to let them throttle it now? And you, my brother
Africans, Mali, Guinea, Ghana, we cry out to you across
our borders. (*Shouting.*) Africa! Do they think Africa
is deaf? Or faint-hearted? Or do they think Africa is
too feeble to deliver us? I know the colonialists are
powerful. But I swear to you by Africa: All of us
united, together, will subdue the monster. Brothers,
already the Congo has won a great victory. We sent
out an appeal to the United Nations and the United
Nations has sent a favorable reply. Tomorrow Mr.
Hammarskjöld, Secretary General of the United Nations, whose integrity and impartiality are recognized
by all, will be with us in Leopoldville. We trust him.
The United Nations will see to it that justice is done.
Full justice.

Gentlemen, I have finished. In a word, our independence, our existence as a nation, our freedom, and
everything that Dependa means to our people are at
stake.

Brothers, I stand here before you, and through you
I look every single Congolese straight in the eye. And
what I have to tell him is best said by our Kikongo
song:

> Brother, in your hand
> You hold what belongs to you.
> Are you going to let another
> Take it away?

You all know the answer. *Kizola ko.* I won't allow it.

DEPUTIES (*rising and shouting*): *Kizola ko. Kizola ko.*

Scene 12

Darkness, then light. In the background a group of European experts take their places around HAMMARSKJÖLD. *They have just landed in Leopoldville after ferrying across the Congo from Brazzaville. The* SANZA PLAYER *crosses the stage, singing:*

> Father Congo
> river of flowers and islands.
> What swells your grey heart
> and shakes it with sobs?

HAMMARSKJÖLD (*to his experts*): Gentlemen, as we set foot for the first time on the soil of the Congo, I am sure that you all share my feeling that this is a profoundly significant moment. The Congo is not only a country, a state, an unhappy state that needs and has asked for our help and protection, it is also a proving ground for the international action that is the aim and ideal of our organization. The work that awaits you here is a great deal more than academic fact-finding. We shall be working for the future of the world.

Gentlemen, in this hour I wish not to sum up my instructions to you, but to define the spirit in which I want you to confront your task here in the Congo.

And I believe that there is no better way of doing so
than to cite the words of the poet:

I recognize no quarrel. I say, let us live,
torch in the wind, flame in the wind,
And in us let all men be so mingled with the flame
    and so consumed
that in the mounting torch a greater light is
    born within us. . .
Tingling the flesh in which the itching soul keeps
    us still rebellious
And it is a time of high fortune when the great
    adventurers of the soul
seek passage on the high road of mankind, ques-
    tioning
the whole threshing floor of the earth, trying to
    discover
the meaning of this vast disorder, questioning
    the bed, the waters of the sky, and the tide-
    marks of the river of shadow on the earth,
perhaps even rebelling at finding no answer . . .

But here come our hosts. Meditate on those words,
gentlemen, meditate on them and find strength in them
as you go forth like a new order of chivalry upon the
high road of humanity.

*The Congolese delegation enters and advances toward
the Europeans.*

Gentlemen of the Congolese government, I am
glad to be here in the Congo at a time when the United
Nations, at your request, has undertaken to help you,
by all the means at its disposal, to lay the foundations
of a happy and prosperous future. Seeing me for the
first time, you must wonder what sort of man I am.
That is only natural. And it's a question I want to
answer. I am a neutral. A good many people think

there's no such animal. But there is, thank the Lord. I am a *neutral*, and I'm here to prove it. The problems confronting the Congo must be solved by conciliation and diplomacy. They cannot be solved by force and intimidation, but only in a spirit of peace and justice. And that is why neutrals can make themselves useful here in the Congo, why they can help to find a satisfactory solution to your problems. For come to think of it, what does the word "neutral" mean? It means "fair," it means "just." And when I say "just," I take the word in the most exacting sense. The just, said Meister Eckhart, "are those who have left their selves behind; who look for nothing above or below or alongside of themselves; who seek neither wealth nor glory nor comfort nor pleasure nor interest nor sanctity nor reward, but have made themselves free from all that."

In short, those who give God their due and through whom God is glorified.

That gentlemen, is the spirit in which we have come among you. To help you to overcome your passions, to bring appeasement to your hearts. To help you to achieve justice and peace. Justice and peace. Those are my words of greeting to the Congo. Long live the Congo!

Scene 13

As the Congolese crowd demonstrates, dancing and singing the "Independence Hot-cha-cha", the AMBASSADOR OF THE GRAND OCCIDENT *steps forward.*

AMBASSADOR: I know my country is getting a bad reputation. They say we're trigger-happy. But is there any room for rocking-chair politics when the world is off its rocker? With people going berserk all over the world, somebody's got to make them behave. And, praise the Lord, Providence has picked us for the job ... You heard what the man said. "To Moscow! To Moscow!" That's what he said. Well, I've got news for you folks. They call us the policemen of the world. Okay. But we're the fire department, too. And it's our job to check the flames of incendiary Communism. Wherever it shows its ugly head. And that includes the Congo. A word to the wise!

ACT 2

Scene 1

The same African bar as in Act I; the GIRLS *and* MAMA
MAKOSI *moving about.* LUMUMBA, MOKUTU, *and friends take
seats.*

LUMUMBA: I like these places . . . I know it upsets the
Pharisees, but . . .

MOKUTU: All the same, it's not going to help our reputation any. Especially abroad. They'll say we're a lot of
sex-crazed apes. Yes, I know. The scenes of your youth,
and all that. But things have changed. We're ministers
and top brass now. You're a Mbota Mutu, a big shot,
and don't forget it.

LUMUMBA: Don't make me laugh. Let the ladies' better-
ment societies turn up their noses. It gives me a kick.
Vice was the only freedom the white men left us.
And then they complain about our morals. Same as the
Americans complain about Harlem . . .

MOKUTU: Maybe so, but you're not seriously thinking of

43

coming here to discuss affairs of state? Hasn't the Congo got a bad enough reputation as it is?

LUMUMBA (*ironically*): Not a bad idea. I'll think it over . . . but now let's talk about something serious. When the Europeans came, the Congo started to disintegrate. It began to rot, piece by piece, and to stink. The state, the family, the people. So maybe this dive with its shady mixed fauna is a faithful reflection of our Congo today. Garbage rotting in the sun. But here and there you see something fresh and new sprouting through the compost. And that's ground for encouragement. (*To* MAMA MAKOSI, *who approaches.*) Well, Mama Makosi, how you doing?

MAMA MAKOSI: Hello, Patrice. Say, we're giving a big freedom ball. Can I count on you? It's going to be terrific: we've rented the Elite Bar.

MOKUTU: Don't be unreasonable, Mama Makosi. Your old friend Patrice is Prime Minister now. You can't expect . . .

MAMA MAKOSI: Oh, come off it. He'll always be the same Patrice for us. Wherever he goes, we'll go. And vice versa. He's not ashamed of his friends.

GIRL: Oh yes, it would be so sweet. I'm the union song leader, and you know what? We're working up a beautiful song. (*She sings.*)

　　When I wear my green bandana . . .

Enter the SANZA PLAYER *disguised as a madman. He passes between the tables, humming.*

MOKUTU: Who's that character?

MAMA MAKOSI: He's just a crazy man. Been coming around for the last few days and we can't get rid of him.

MOKUTU: Can't you call the police?

LUMUMBA: Leave the poor man alone. He isn't bothering anybody.

SANZA PLAYER (*declaiming*): Ah, God of the Christians! Why did you let the white men go away . . . ?

MOKUTU: Get a load of that. He can't live without his daily ration of kicks. He's an addict.

LUMUMBA: No, Mokutu, it's worse than that . . . It takes a lot of thinking to face the truth that God is dead. Our country people . . .

SANZA PLAYER: Oh God, why did you make black men so wicked?

MOKUTU: Good grief!

SANZA PLAYER: I came down the river, looking for the white men who left my village, and I didn't find them; the white men left our village and the black men are wicked. The black men are cursed . . .

LUMUMBA: See, Mokutu? It's useful to hang around these places. That's the bitter truth of our Congo. That's the disease we've got to cure our people of. Mama Makosi, I want to thank you and your bar for this lesson. And don't worry, you can count on me, I'll come to your ball, and I'll bring my Cabinet. (*They exit.*)

SANZA PLAYER: Let's throw off this mask. I've said enough. I've done enough. Even if a man has good eyes, you've got to show him certain things. But he'll see the rest for himself. And it's plain enough to see. It doesn't take a hurricane to part a chicken's tail feathers.

Scene 2

A meeting of the Congolese cabinet. LUMUMBA, MPOLO, MOKUTU, CROULARD (*Lumumba's Belgian secretary*), *and others.*

LUMUMBA: Gentlemen, that is the situation. There's no time to lose. We're in the midst of a battle. On every front. The survival of the Congo is at stake.

CROULARD: I beg your pardon, Your Excellency, but Mr. Bunche, the Assistant Secretary of the United Nations, wants to see you. He says it's urgent.

LUMUMBA: Who told him to come here? Who sent for him? But never mind, Croulard, as long as you've interrupted us, pass me the file on the district chiefs . . . And another thing, gentlemen, we've got to take up the question of visas. All sorts of people are coming in without visas. Or worse, with Belgian visas.

CROULARD: Your Excellency, Mr. Bunche is very insistent. He says . . .

LUMUMBA: Croulard! Will you kindly let us work? (*He rushes to the phone.*) Hello. Stanleyville? Is that you, Jean? . . . All right, arrange the meeting. I'll speak . . . I can tell you right now, there's going to be some excitement. We're going to abolish the district militias

46

and mobilize the unemployed. Hello? Oh yes, I'd forgotten. Don't forget to order beer . . . by the carload . . . Enough for the whole population . . . Good-bye. (*He hangs up.*)

Enter ISAAC KALONJI.

ISAAC: Howdy! Howdy, everybody . . . All that's fine and dandy, my dear Prime Minister. But when are we going into Katanga? What are we waiting for? All you've got to do is make a beeline for Bakwanga! Our partisans will rise up . . . Albert Kalonji has taken it on the lam . . . Tzumbi is saying his prayers . . .

MPOLO: I agree with Isaac. We need Bakwanga. That's where the diamonds are. And what's a crown without diamonds?

LUMUMBA: We need. We need. Just get me some planes. But don't worry, Isaac, I'm attending to it.

MOKUTU: Not just planes, Mr. Prime Minister . . . troops . . . no money, no troops. That's the way soldiers are, and they haven't been paid in two months.

LUMUMBA: All right, all right. We'll give you money.

MOKUTU: Thank you. But you haven't heard the last of my complaints. I won't stand for amateurishness. You made me a colonel, I'm going to be a real colonel.

LUMUMBA: What's on your mind?

MOKUTU: Well, I hear that Mpolo has been going around with a colonel's cap and a swagger stick . . . The government will have to choose between us. It's either him or me.

LUMUMBA: Come, come, Mokutu, there's nothing to get excited about . . . you were away on a tour of inspection. We thought it wise to appoint Mpolo a colonel too.

In this situation two of you aren't too many. If you're not satisfied, we can appoint you general and Mpolo can be chief of staff.

Hubbub among the ministers.

SANZA PLAYER: That's it . . . A good compromise. Now everybody will be happy.

MOKUTU: I'm sorry. I'm telling you plainly. The army isn't an operetta. I'd rather resign.

LUMUMBA: All right. Mokutu remains chief of staff. As for you, Mpolo, we'll see later on. Meanwhile, take off that uniform. Well, Croulard, what about that file on the district chiefs? All those petty potentates, those police dogs who helped the Belgians to crush our people. If we want real leaders, we've got to get rid of them first. And where do you find real leaders except among the common people? Well, Croulard, how about that file?

CROULARD: I can't find it, Your Excellency . . . This place is such a mess. Well, here at least is a big bundle I wasn't looking for . . . I open it, and what do I see? Guess. A bundle of telegrams. Messages from twenty nations or more, recognizing the Republic of the Congo. And nobody's read them. Been here for two weeks. It's a mess, I tell you. A mess.

LUMUMBA: Luckily we have you, Croulard, to make a little order.

MOKUTU (*grumbling*): And to poke his nose into a lot of things that are none of his business.

MPOLO: Comrade Prime Minister, we were speaking of Katanga just now. Maybe if we can't take Katanga for the moment, we could at least take Leopoldville. The Abako youth organization are acting as if they owned the streets. Agitating against us under our own windows.

MOKUTU: Careful, gentlemen. A blow at the Abako is a blow at the President.

LUMUMBA: Mpolo, you're the youth minister, aren't you? Why can't you set up your own youth organization? The NCM Youth Brigade. Every time the Abako demonstrates, you stage a counter-demonstration. That'll do it. You don't need government intervention for that.

MPOLO: Okay, chief!

Enter the CHIEF OF POLICE.

Well, well, here comes my police force. What news?

CHIEF OF POLICE: Excellency, another article by Gabriel Makoso in *Christian Conscience.* A diatribe by Monsignor Malula . . . and leaflets, millions of leaflets!

LUMUMBA: Never mind the leaflets. I know them by heart: Lumumba has mortgaged the Congo to the Russians, Lumumba has sold his soul to the Devil, Lumumba has received millions from the Czech Ambassador. (*Taking the newspaper.*) This is more serious. (*He glances through it.*) Oh, oh! Monsignor doesn't pull his punches. Hmm. Read it to us, Mpolo.

MPOLO (*reading*): "And first and foremost we must denounce anticlericalism, that waste-product of the Occident, imported into the Congo by unworthy rulers. To arms against the enemies of religion wherever they may be, the Freemasons like Makessa, the self-styled atheists like the ignominious Lumumba!"

LUMUMBA: Not bad for a bishop. The ignominious Lumumba! Well, he's going to hear from the ignominious Lumumba. They want war? All right, they'll get it.

   Mr. Police Chief, do your duty. You will arrest Makoso and shut his paper down.

MOKUTU: I beg your pardon, Mr. Prime Minister. Isn't that unwise? Won't it make for unrest?

LUMUMBA: Watch your step, Mokutu . . . stick to your own department. You're in charge of the army. I've agreed to that. Politics is my business. And don't worry about the unrest, I'll know how to deal with it . . . Gentlemen, we can strike, or we can let ourselves be struck down. I have made up my mind: We will strike.

I demand that Lundula be given full powers: the army will arrest everyone, white or black, who attempts to stir up trouble. No half-measures. No hesitation. Which reminds me, the Abako is making too much noise. They've scheduled a congress in Thysville. They're talking secession. Another secession. Well, there's not going to be any congress. Their congress is cancelled. Come to think of it, they haven't a leg to stand on. The law requires two weeks' notice. They didn't give it . . . Agreed, gentlemen?

MPOLO: Agreed. The law is the law. No special privileges.

LUMUMBA: As for Katanga, Isaac is right. That's our main problem . . . the key to all our other problems . . . I'll see Hammarskjöld . . . The United Nations is here to help us . . . You'll get your planes, Mokutu, you'll get your planes. As Isaac says, Tzumbi had better say his prayers.

The SANZA PLAYER *passes, singing:*

> Sun and rain
> Driving rain
> Rising sun
> The elephant
> Begets a son.

Scene 3

Lumumba's office.

LUMUMBA: Mr. Secretary General, I appealed to the United Nations. I was the first chief of state to put full trust in your organization. Who would have thought that my first words to you would be words not of thanks but of reproach and recrimination. Please believe that I deeply regret it. But unfortunately you have put a very personal interpretation on the resolutions of the Security Council: the Belgians are still in the Congo. And the United Nations is holding diplomatic conversations with the traitor Tzumbi.

HAMMARSKJÖLD: I am the Secretary General of the United Nations Organization. I am responsible solely to the General Assembly. I owe you no accounts. But I can tell you this much: I have no orders to massacre the people of Katanga.

LUMUMBA: You have called off the military operations that would have enabled us to enter Elisabethville without striking a blow.

HAMMARSKJÖLD: If I called them off, or postponed them, it was because Bunche's reports left no room for doubt: it would have been necessary to fight for every street, for every house in Elisabethville.

51

LUMUMBA: Nonsense. The population of Katanga are only waiting to throw off Tzumbi's yoke. They would have welcomed you as a liberator. But you saw fit to confer with the rebel . . .

HAMMARSKJÖLD: Mr. Prime Minister, I followed the dictates of my conscience. It is a point of doctrine, a point of my doctrine, that the UN must not participate in an internal conflict, constitutional or otherwise, and that its armed forces cannot be utilized in such conflicts. I am not saying there is no problem. There is. But it is a problem that I do not despair of solving. President Tzumbi has impressed me as a sensible man. I shall make every effort to reason with him and convince him. In any case, this country has suffered enough. I have no desire to add a full-scale war to its misfortunes.

LUMUMBA: I appreciate your solicitude. But tell me, what greater misfortune can there be for this country than the secession of its richest province? You speak of resistance in Katanga. Tzumbi and Msiri must have had a good laugh. They had already rented houses for themselves in Rhodesia. Your Bunche is as gullible as a child. He misjudged the situation. Unless . . . After all, Bunche is an American . . .

HAMMARSKJÖLD: That has nothing to do with it. I permit no one to cast aspersions on the honesty and impartiality of my co-workers. I am a neutral, surrounded by neutrals who put the interest of the world at large before any consideration deriving from their own personal nationality.

LUMUMBA: I leave it to history to judge that. In any event, since the UN has failed to meet its obligations, to carry out its mission, the government of the Congolese Republic will assume its responsibilities. We will re-

duce the secession of Katanga by force. Our troops are
ready. The campaign must be concluded before the
rainy season. I trust that the UN will not refuse to
lend me a certain number of planes to transport our
armed forces.

HAMMARSKJÖLD: Planes? I thought I had made it clear
to you that the United Nations troops are by definition
a peace force, not a force of aggression.

LUMUMBA: There you have it, that's the impartiality of the
UN. Every day Belgian arms and mercenaries pour
into the Congo. And you just look on.

HAMMARSKJÖLD: You are unjust. I have addressed a strong
note of protest on the subject to the Brussels government.

LUMUMBA: A note! Yes, a note. And meanwhile the secessionists are building up their forces. Everybody knows
it, and what do you do? You not only refuse to take
action, but you prevent us from acting. Very well! The
Congo will do without your help. We still have a few
friends in the world. We will manage without you
neutrals.

HAMMARSKJÖLD: I wish to remind you that all foreign aid
to the Congo must pass through United Nations chan-
nels.

LUMUMBA: You don't do things by halves, Mr. Secretary
General. Very well, but permit me in turn to remind
you that it is a point of doctrine, a point of my doctrine, that the Congo is an independent country and
that we haven't shaken off Belgian rule in order to
accept the rule of the United Nations. Good day, Mr.
Secretary General. The Russians will lend me the
planes that you refuse me. In a few days we shall be
in Elisabethville. As for you, whatever may happen,

I hope you will not one day pay too dearly for your illusions.

HAMMARSKJÖLD: Mr. Lumumba, I learned one thing long ago: to say *yes* to Destiny, whatever it may be. But since we are exchanging good wishes, I hope that whatever may befall, you will not one day have to pay too dearly for your imprudence and impulsiveness . . . Good-bye.

The SANZA PLAYER *passes, singing:*

> A magpie on a cherry tree
> Preens himself and plays the peacock,
> Saying "This tree belongs to me."
> Oh, let me die in poverty
> If riches means a magpie's tree.

Scene 4

Darkness, then half-light. Alarming noises. Gradually, as in a nightmare, groups appear: women, witches, warriors armed with spears and blowguns. A voice rises, the VOICE OF CIVIL WAR.

CIVIL WAR:

> Boy, pour the palm wine.
> Hot and spicy,
> Thick muddy dregs.
> Pour the palm wine. When I'm drunk, I ask
> For my sword, my sharpened sword that hangs
> On the wall with buffalo horn and *assegai.*
> Pour the palm wine, boy!
> When I'm drunk, I take down my bow that hangs
> on the wall with my war horn and *assegai.*
> Boy, by day I'll fight
> and at night, I'll praise my bow,
> I'll honor it with a branch of wild grape.
> I'll rub it with oil at night,
> At night it deserves to shine like a mirror.
> Boy! My machete!
> A brave man isn't made to die in his bed,
> A brave man is an elephant,
> A spitting serpent.
> Palm wine man, pour the wine, color of enemy
> blood.

When the day returns, we'll face
The enemy eye to eye.
Boy! Pour the palm wine.
I'm drunk! On wine? On enemy blood? I don't
    know.
The spear is in my hands. Eiii!
The spear strikes and bends in the wound!
Enemy head, I'll display you in every village.

Scene 5

Meeting of the Congolese Cabinet.

LUMUMBA: Gentlemen, I've got big news for you. Our troops have taken Bakwanga. The traitor Kalonji has fled.

KALA: A victory, unfortunately, that may cost us more than a defeat.

FIRST MINISTER: I see what you mean, and I share your sentiments. We've got to admit that our army has had a heavy hand. Six thousand Balubas killed. In the church of Saint-Jean of Bakwanga forty Baluba families massacred with the most atrocious cruelty.

SECOND MINISTER: I demand that the army be recalled.

THIRD MINISTER: Our army has dishonored us in the eyes of the world.

LUMUMBA: Poor Balubas! Massacred by our soldiers in Kasai! Exterminated by Tzumbi's police in Katanga! They've been called the Jews of Africa. But a military campaign is never a battle of flowers.

KALA: We're in a pretty mess all the same. The world press is up in arms against us. Especially the Belgian papers. And Hammarskjöld is raising hell in the UN. He accuses us of genocide.

LUMUMBA: He does, does he? And where was Hammarskjöld when the Belgians were massacring our men and
raping our women?

And now we're the savages!

So the Belgians are complaining? That's a good one.
And who stirred up the Luluas against the Balubas?
Who made the Balubas think the Luluas were getting
ready to murder them? Who invented chief Kalamba
Mangole and started him plugging for a Lulua king-
dom that would drive out the Balubas unless they sub-
mitted to the laws and customs of the Luluas? Who
persuaded the Balubas and Luluas that they couldn't
coexist anymore? In 1959. You remember? And what
did the Belgian police do while they were cutting
each other's throats? They looked on and smiled. And
where was Lumumba then? In prison. And what about
the Christian, civilized world press? What did it
have to say then? And the world conscience? No! Do
they think I'm going to let the Congo be torn limb
from limb for fear of their hypocritical protests?
Gentlemen, I reject your authority. (*He laughs.*) I reject your law, your morality, your whole system! Yes,
my friends, let us celebrate. I want every Congolese
citizen to drink a glass of beer to the capture of Bakwanga.

Tonight I'm going to make a speech on the radio to
celebrate the taking of Bakwanga. Mpolo, we'll go to
the Elite Bar tonight. No, to Cassian's. I know a Lulua
girl. She's beautiful. Her name is Hélène Jewel. And
she certainly is a jewel. Get in touch with her. I'm
going to dance with her tonight. With a Lulua girl.
In the eyes of the whole world.

And you, gentlemen of the press and pulpit, champ-
ions of the world conscience, I expect you to light up
the dance floor with your grimaces.

Scene 6

Cassian's Bar. LUMUMBA *and* HÉLÈNE JEWEL, *dancing in a pink and green half-light.*

HÉLÈNE:

> I dance things of cavernous darkness
> blood's fire, keen snakes
> caught in the brambles of exile.

LUMUMBA:

> I dance the sprouting of man and his saliva, salt.
> And alone in the depths of his aloneness man sickens
>   at
> the taste of his flesh, insipid cassava.

HÉLÈNE:

> I dance the pavonia flower that wheels around the sun,
>   when
> every flick of the planet's lashes brightens the smooth
>   purple
> of the living blood.

LUMUMBA:

> I dance the high vessel that with its blazoned prow
>   governs
> the panic of Desire; the pavonia bird and its pavan.

HÉLÈNE:

> I dance the joy, sown by the sun, of the incongruous
>   small

rain planting its dispersed copper laughter in the
  briny flesh
of the sea.

LUMUMBA:

I dance the insect, more beautiful than any name,
  which in the
core of the ripe fruit established its glutted weariness,
  gold and
jade and obsidian.

HÉLÈNE:

And now our dance is danced, the refrain closes its
  corolla as,
proud to have sustained the unsustainable, ablaze and
  slaked with
fire, the pavonia flower closes.

LUMUMBA:

We have danced the dance of my life! When I am
  gone, when I
am spent like the blinding blind meteor in the night
  sky,
when the Congo is no more than a season seasoned
  with blood,
be beautiful, still beautiful, keeping
of the terrible days no more
than the few drops of dew that make
the hummingbird's plumes more beautiful
for having traversed the storm.
No sadness, darling. Dance with me till dawn
and give me heart
to go on to the end of the night.

Scene 7

A room in the President's palace. KALA *is alone.*

KALA: All I hear about is blood. Blood and horror. The Luluas killing the Balubas. The Balubas exterminating the Luluas. And our army, the National Army of the Congo, massacring everybody in sight.

Oh, this war! this war!

Yes, yes, I gave my consent. But do you think it's easy to say no to that goateed devil? Anyway, it was his decision. Let him take the consequences.

He's too highhanded.

That incident with the UN soldiers, for instance. Bunche wants to see him about it, Lumumba refers him to some undersecretary. Naturally—what would you expect—Bunche ends up in my office. What could I say? Nobody tells me anything, I said. And it's true. He doesn't tell me anything . . . What does he take me for? A figurehead? To tell the truth, he's a strange man. I'll never get used to him. Sometimes he's so sensitive, so full of fine feeling. I remember what he said to me before leaving for New York. "President, I leave you my heart."

"I leave you my heart." There was real friendship in those words. They came from the heart . . . Ah, what a man!

Maybe that's what I hold against him most, his impulsiveness. Always so agitated, so excited. A ball of fire! A hammerbird, always looking for somebody to ram his head into.

Our ancestors were right, a real chief doesn't get excited. He doesn't run around in circles. He is immobile and enduring. He concentrates. He is the concentrated essence of the country. And by concentrating, he emanates a gentle persuasive light . . . This fellow's a hothead. He doesn't emanate, he just sets everything on fire. He's a *Kintu-Kintu!* He'd turn the whole country upside down if I let him. He'd set the Congo on fire and the world with it. But I am here and I won't let him. I'm here to save the Congo and to save him from himself. Easy does it, Patrice. Go easy. Old Kala's here. He's here all right. And here to stay. They call me the old man. I'm not old. I'm slow. They say the tortoise is full of guile. Full of good sense would be more like it. I make my way slowly; slowly, *Kukutu Bvem, Kukutu Bvem.** And he's impetuous, a hothead.

I don't like hotheads even when they're right. They make me dizzy. And besides, sooner or later, they wear themselves out . . . But that's enough daydreaming. I've got to write this speech.

Actually I don't see why they all hound him so. But whom don't they hound? Ah, it's a bad world nowadays. They say Patrice leads me by the nose. They say I betrayed the Bakongo by accepting the presidency. They even dare to write: "Kala is Lumumba's woman." "Kala is Lumumba's wife."

That's stupid. A president is the chief. He's the king. Besides, I can dismiss him whenever I please. The constitution says so. The president makes the decisions, the ministers carry them out. Of course I don't

---

* Onomatopoeia for the slow, deliberate movement of a turtle.

mean to make use of my power. Patrice is intelligent, energetic, popular. Oh yes, he's popular all right. They can slander him all they like, they can't stop him from being popular. And there's strength in popularity.

And I've got to take it into consideration . . . But why in God's name are they all out to get him? Look what they've thought up now: Patrice is a communist. And by protecting him, I'm giving aid and comfort to the Communist International.

That's nonsense. Patrice a communist! I remember the look on his face that time, in the midst of our worst trouble with the Belgians, when I suggested a telegram to Khrushchev. Do you know what he said? "It's impossible, Mr. President. They're already saying that I've sold out to the communists. That would clinch it. You're a Christian, you can do it if you want to. And even so, they'll say I maneuvered you."

Hm . . . Maneuvered me? That would take quite a man. Quite a man. But it's true. He is quite a man. The American ambassador said to me last week: "If Lumumba went into a meeting of Congolese politicians with a tray, disguised as a waiter, he'd be prime minister by the time he left." But do they think it's so easy to fool old Kala . . . Do they really? . . . I'd better consult Bishop Malula. He's got a head on his shoulders . . . And I'll ask Mokutu to go with me . . . (*He laughs.*) I could have been a bishop myself . . . Why . . . we were at the seminary together . . .As a bishop I'd have had fewer worries, that's sure . . . But no man chooses his fate . . . Oh Lord, oh Lord. Oh, this presidency! . . . Well, how about it? Am I going to write that speech? Come along, Kala. Make a little effort. (*He starts to work.*)

The SANZA PLAYER *enters, singing:*

Thoughts come in sudden flashes
I see the croaking frog
The chameleon on his branch
Waiting with darting tongue.

Scene 8

Lumumba's apartment. LUMUMBA *and his wife*, PAULINE.

PAULINE: Patrice, I'm afraid. Oh God! I can feel the knives of hatred in the darkness, and everywhere I see termites, toads, spiders, the crawling vermin of envy. Patrice, I can see their filthy plots tightening around you...

LUMUMBA: What is there to be afraid of? It's true I have enemies... but the people are for me. The people are my shield. I speak to them and they understand me, they follow me. This is a revolution, Pauline, and in a revolution it's the people that count.

PAULINE: The people, yes. But the people are weak and disarmed. They're credulous. And your enemies are sly and patient, and they've got the whole world behind them.

LUMUMBA: Don't exaggerate... I have friends, too... faithful friends. We stick together... We're like a dog's hairs, all in the same bed.

PAULINE: Friends, friends!... I can think of a dozen of them who owe you everything. They dance attendance, but they're only waiting for the chance to knife you. Some of them would sell you for a mess of pottage. I feel it in my bones.

LUMUMBA: Oh, you women. So cynical. Always fearing the worst.

PAULINE: And you men? And you yourself? So innocent and so trusting. You're a child, Patrice . . . For instance, I don't trust your Mokuto . . . I don't have to tell you that he was an informer for the Belgians . . .

LUMUMBA: I know, I know that, Pauline . . . But I also know what the situation was in those days. A lot of people had no other choice than to starve and let their children starve or to play the stoolpigeon. It's not pretty, no, it's not pretty. But some of the people who disgraced themselves in those days can be saved . . . And Mokutu is one of them . . . He's intelligent, shrewd . . . not much character, but he's grateful to me for my confidence in him . . . My confidence helps him to redeem himself in his own eyes . . . I can answer for his loyalty.

PAULINE: God protect you, Patrice. God protect you.

LUMUMBA: And besides, what can he do to me? . . . Stop worrying . . . They can't hurt me as long as Kala and I stick together, and we always will.

PAULINE: Are you so sure, Patrice? I have an idea that he's jealous of you . . .

PATRICE: I repeat: never have two men seen more eye to eye than Kala and I . . . He has his faults, but he's a patriot . . . He's the chief of a powerful tribe, an excellent tribe, the Bakongo! And remember the proverb: Look at the cock's beak and you'll see the whole cock.

PAULINE: All the same. So many people are trying to make trouble between you . . . He's secretive . . . sly . . . You just be careful. Sitting on his throne as rigid and serene as a copper god, all he seems to think of right now is holding his scepter up. But when the time comes, he's perfectly capable, if you ask me, of bringing it down on your head—without a word of warning.

LUMUMBA: And you think I'm so easy to crush? You think I have no weapons, no friends . . . But we've talked enough, Pauline . . . I'm tired, give me my guitar. (*She gives him the guitar.*) I don't know why . . . I've got this sad tune running through my head . . . It's a Swahili song. Ever heard it, Pauline?

The lights are slowly dimmed as he sings.

> Would you lean
> Even your finger
> On a rotting tree?
> Life is a rotting tree.
> Don't lean, don't lean
> Even a finger
> On the rotting tree.

LUMUMBA (*yawning*): Ah! Dependa wears you out! (*He dozes off, then wakes with a start.*) What's this?

In his nightmare a BISHOP, KALA, and MOKUTU appear stage front. KALA and MOKUTU are kneeling.

BISHOP: My children, the time has come to prove your love for the Church and to chastise the enemies of our holy religion. The Church is relying on you. In the name of the Father, the Son, and the Holy Ghost, amen.

PAULINE: Poor Patrice. Wake up. It's almost time for the news. (*She turns the radio dial, a speech by KALA LUBU is heard.*)

KALA: My dear compatriots, I have an important announcement to make: The Mayor, I beg your pardon, the Prime Minister, I mean, who was appointed by the

King of Belgium in accordance with the provisional constitution, has betrayed his trust. He has taken arbitrary measures which have provoked dissension among the government and the people. He has deprived many citizens of their basic liberties. He has plunged the country into an abominable civil war. In view of all this, I have esteemed it necessary to dissolve the government. I have appointed Joseph Ileo Prime Minister and empowered him to form a new government. I have already assured myself of the total and wholehearted support of our glorious Congolese army and of its commander, Colonel Mokutu. I hope and trust that I can also count on the discipline and patriotism of the entire Congolese people. God protect the Congo!

Scene 9

Lumumba's office that same evening. Enter MPOLO *in haste, a moment later* LUMUMBA.

LUMUMBA: The bastard. But he hasn't heard the last of Patrice Lumumba. President of the Republic! Who made him President of the Republic?

But maybe it's all for the best, Mpolo. The Congo of the provisional constitution, the two-headed monster born of the fornications at the Round Table, was a compromise. I accepted it only as a temporary evil. And now King Kala, on his own initiative, has shown that the time for compromise has passed.

So much the better. The time has come to get rid of King Kala. Notify the radio station. I am going to address the nation.

MPOLO: You're right. It's time for us to strike. But what about the UN? Will they be neutral?

LUMUMBA: The UN? The UN is a fiction. What exists, regardless of the color of their helmets, is men, soldiers from all over Africa. And luckily for us, the radio station is in the hands of the Ghanaians. A soldier of Nkrumah isn't going to refuse aid and comfort to Lumumba. Send for Ghana!

Scene 10

The Radio Building.

LUMUMBA: I'm glad to see you, Colonel. Ghana is a great country, dear to the hearts of all true Africans. I for my part shall never forget that it was in Ghana— thanks to Nkrumah—that the African first threw off the chains of colonialism and stood up a free man.

GHANA: Independence is one thing, disorder is another. And that is what I see in the Congo.

LUMUMBA: We shall overcome it, Colonel, and you will help us. I trust that Mpolo has given you my message. The people are in need of explanations and directives. I will speak on the radio tonight.

GHANA: So I have heard, Mr. Lumumba. Unfortunately, Monsieur Cordelier, the United Nations delegate in Leopoldville, has given strict orders: all political activity in the Congo is suspended until further notice, and no member of any political faction is to be given access to the radio.

LUMUMBA: So now Cordelier is giving orders in the Congo! But let it pass . . . In any case, his orders don't apply to me. I shall address the country not as President of the National Congo Movement but as Prime Minister.

GHANA: Mr. Lumumba, we have a proverb in our country: "The state is an egg. Squeeze it too tight and it will break; not tight enough, and it will fall and smash." I don't know whether you have squeezed too tight or not tight enough, but the fact is that there is no longer a Congolese state.

LUMUMBA: Am I to understand that you, on your own responsibility, deny me the use of my country's radio?

GHANA: I am only a soldier, sir. I carry out orders.

LUMUMBA: Oh, oh! Perhaps you didn't realize, colonel, that your president is my friend? That Ghana, more than an ally, is our brother country? That the government in Accra has promised me its total and unconditional support? Your cowardice and insolence leaves me aghast. And I warn you that I shall not fail to inform your president, my friend, Kwame Nkrumah.

GHANA: Sir, here in the Congo I am not in the service of Ghana, but of the United Nations. I am a soldier, sir, not a politician. As for my relations with Nkrumah, the two of us will straighten that out when the time comes, without your help. You have enough to do in the Congo.

LUMUMBA: I understand. You call yourself a soldier. No, I'll tell you what you are. You're just one more traitor.
Nkrumah wrote me: "Brother, you must keep as cool as a cucumber." He's right. Treason is worse than toad venom, worse than the scaly pangolin coiled around its branch. To keep calm in the presence of an African traitor I'd need to have water in my veins like a Ghanaian cucumber, not Congolese blood.

GHANA (*drawing his revolver*): Everybody knows that a man who sets foot in this lousy country has to be prepared for anything. But there's one thing I'll never put up with, less in this filthy Congo than anywhere else, and that's the insolence of a half-baked communist.

LUMUMBA: Fire! Go ahead and fire! You see that I'm as cool as a cucumber.

GHANA (*returning his pistol to its holster*): Come to think of it, no ... The Congolese will attend to it themselves.

Exit GHANA, *enter the* SANZA PLAYER *and* MOKUTU *with a detachment of paratroopers.*

SANZA PLAYER: Fellow Africans, that's the tragedy. A hunter catches sight of a crowned stork in the tree top. Luckily the tortoise has seen the hunter. The stork is saved, you will say. And indeed, the tortoise tells the big leaf, who's supposed to tell the creeper, who's supposed to tell the bird. Oh no! It's everybody for himself. Result: the hunter kills the bird, takes the big leaf to wrap the bird in, and cuts the creeper to tie up the leaf ... And oh yes, I forgot. He even walks off with the tortoise. Africans, my brothers! When will you understand?

Scene 11

Lumumba's home, occupied by Mokutu's paratroopers.

LUMUMBA: Thank you for coming. I'm glad you recognize that I am entitled to an explanation.

MOKUTU: There's nothing to explain. Civil war, foreign war, anarchy. Patrice, I'm afraid you're a luxury the Congo can't afford.

LUMUMBA: Can you be sincere? Do you really think you're saving the Congo? Doesn't it occur to you that by wrecking our constitutional government before we've even had time to set it up, you are endangering the very life of your country.

MOKUTU: You'd have made things easier for us by stepping down of your own accord. But that's too much to expect of a politician. I have no other course than to dismiss you. But the old man is mistaken. I'm dismissing him too . . . I've decided to neutralize the government.

LUMUMBA: When I hear big words like that, I can't help smelling a rat. Exactly what are you driving at?

MOKUTU: It's perfectly simple. The President fires the Prime Minister. The Prime Minister strikes back and fires the President. I'm firing both of you. We're sick of politicians.

LUMUMBA: In other words, you've decided to seize power.
Well, after all, you won't be the first colonel to stage
a coup d'état. But watch your step, Mokutu. The day
when every discontented officer feels entitled to make
a grab for power, there won't be much left of our country. A gang of thieves is no substitute for a state.

MOKUTU: Don't you dare to impugn my honesty. I am a
soldier and always will be. I have appointed a com-
mittee of specialists to run the government until order
is restored. Meanwhile I'm calling off the civil war. I
have ordered the army to suspend operations against
Kasai. There's plenty of work to do right here in
Leopoldville.

LUMUMBA: Mokutu, I won't remind you of our friendship,
of the struggles we've been through together, but . . .

MOKUTU: No, there's no point in talking about the past.
Sure. I helped you to get out of prison. I was with
you at the Round Table conference in Brussels. I cam-
paigned for you day and night. Five years of friendship. But I refuse to let friendship interfere with my
duty as a citizen and a Congolese patriot. This is the
parting of the ways. It's my duty to neutralize you.

LUMUMBA: You're right, this is no time for personal senti-
ment. But have you ever stopped to think about
Africa? Look here. No need of a wall map, it's en-
graved in the palm of my hand.

Here's Northern Rhodesia; its heart is the Copper
Belt. A silent country, except for a foreman's curses
now and then, the bark of a police dog, the burbling
of a Colt—they've gunned down a black man, who
drops without a word. Look here, next door. Southern
Rhodesia. Millions of Negroes robbed, dispossessed,
herded into the so-called townships.

And here's Angola. What's its main article of ex-

port? Not sugar, not coffee, but slaves. Yes, colonel,
slaves. Two hundred thousand men a year sent to the
mines of South Africa in exchange for good money to
help replenish Papa Salazar's empty treasury.

And dangling from it like a rag, this little island,
this rock, San Tomé, devouring niggers by the thousand, by the million. Africa's penal colony. (*He sings.*)

> They took our boy away,
> Sent him to San Tomé
> 'Cause he had no card,
> Aié
> He never came back 'cause death
> Took him away,
> Aié
> They sent him to San Tomé.

Funny you never heard that song. I'll teach it to you,
Mokutu, if you give me time. Well, further down
there's South Africa, the racist slave camp, with its
tanks and planes, its Bible, its laws, its courts, its
press, its hatred, its lies—its hard, cruel heart. That's
our Africa, Mokutu. Prostrate, bound, trampled, a tar-
get for white men's guns. But there's hope, you'll say.
They suffer, but they hope. And it's true. Because deep
down in their dungeon, like a diver deep under the sea,
they see a spot of light on the surface, a spot of light,
growing, growing. Why shouldn't they hope? There's
been Ghana, Guinea, Senegal, Mali . . . Dahomey,
Cameroun. Not so long ago, Togoland. And now the
Congo. And imprisoned Africa says to itself: "Tomorrow will be my turn. Tomorrow isn't so far off." And
they clench their fists and breathe a little freer. The
air of tomorrow, the good salt air of freedom.

Mokutu, do you know what you're doing? You're
blacking out the little patch of light over the prisoner's

cell. The great rainbow bird is wheeling over the cells of a hundred and fifty million men; at both ends of the horizon the double serpent is rearing up, bearing promise of life, a hope of life and sky. But with one stroke of your stupid club you strike it down, and the scaly coils of malignant darkness come down on the whole continent.

MOKUTU: I won't follow you in your apocalypse. I'm not responsible for Africa but for the Congo. And in the Congo I mean to restore order. Order, do you understand? Order.

The SOLDIERS *have come in silently and occupy the whole stage.*

ACT 3

Scene 1

Camp Hardy in Thysville. A prison cell. MPOLO, OKITO, *and* LUMUMBA *on narrow cots. Morning.* LUMUMBA *tossing and moaning in his sleep.*

LUMUMBA: Oh! Oh!

OKITO: He's got one of his nightmares again.

MPOLO: Poor Patrice. He's struggling like a fly caught in syrup.

LUMUMBA (*waking up and rubbing his eyes*): There's no way out! What a dream! Big ferocious birds were attacking me from all directions, I was thrashing around like a madman trying to defend myself. It was awful.

OKITO: The proverb says: We eat with the sun, not with the moon. I don't like dreams.

LUMUMBA: I do, even when they're terrible. There's wisdom in them. We forget it too soon when we wake up.

MPOLO: I know. I know. Our ancestors! You can have

them. Right now they're kind of stingy with their
favors.

OKITO: Yes, they've forgotten us in the bitter savannah.

LUMUMBA: Courage, friends. The people were taken by
surprise, but they're pulling themselves together now.
You know the legend. We'll sacrifice Lumumba, the
gods will be appeased and smile on the Congo. Sure.
Things will pick up . . . The Belgians will disarm,
Tzumbi will return to the fold, the UN will pour
in aid by the shipload, and so on. But friends, it
doesn't work. Things are going from bad to worse.
Waste, disorder, anarchy, corruption, humiliation.
You'll see, it won't be long before they come begging
us to take the reins again.

MPOLO: Unless to eliminate that possibility they decide to
do away with us first. Something tells me they're not
going to stop halfway. We never do in the Congo.

OKITO: The Congo, the Congo! The international bankers,
you mean. They're touchy. At the slightest poke they
go out of their minds. The buffalo, that's what it is,
the buffalo.

MPOLO: When the buffalo shits, the whole world stinks.

LUMUMBA: All that is true; our life is at the mercy of the
first killer on the payroll. Black or white, it's all the
same. If he's black, a white man has sent him. Yes, they
can destroy us, but they can't defeat us. It's too late.
We've got the jump on them. History will leave them
behind.

MPOLO: You certainly are a prophet, Patrice. You march
ahead and proclaim the future. That's your strength
and your weakness.

LUMUMBA: Part praise, part blame, I accept that verdict,

Mpolo. Especially if it can infect you with my unshakable faith in the future.

MPOLO: Yes, part praise and part blame. Sometimes I wonder if we weren't trying to go too fast.

LUMUMBA: I regret nothing, Mpolo. Does an architect project half a house? No, he plans the whole house at once. When the sky was black and there was no horizon in sight, wasn't it necessary to show the way with one magic stroke?

And let's not underestimate our strength. It's enormous. We've just got to know how to use it. Look, here are two letters I've just received, that escaped the vigilance of Mokutu's thugs. One's from Van Laert, the other's from Luis. Isn't it marvelous? Luis, a Spaniard! Why should he be interested in the Congo? After all, those people have their own problems. And Van Laert. A Belgian. My friend, my brother in Brussels. I bet you he's thinking of me right now, this very minute, same as I'm thinking of him. Those people are with us. They're with us because they know that the battle we're fighting isn't for ourselves, or even for Africa, but for all mankind. And Africa. Yes, I know, it's divided, it seems to be weak, but it won't fail us. Wasn't it here in Africa, from the solemn encounter of muck, sun, and water, that man was born? What is man but a certain way of dispelling the mists of life, by standing erect and holding the head high? All right, Mpolo, I'll talk to the soldiers, they're Congolese, I'll break their hearts. (*To the* JAILERS *and* SOLDIERS.) Well, comrade jailers, how about a glass of beer? But I'm sorry, all I've got is Polar.

JAILER: Don't let that worry you, boss. Primus or Polar, it's all the same to us. We won't argue about the brand, we're too damn thirsty.

LUMUMBA: Drink, friends. And how's the country getting along?

JAILER: The country? Nothing's changed. People are beginning to wonder if Dependa isn't a swarm of grasshoppers come to ruin us.

LUMUMBA: Let's not blame Dependa for what her enemies do. But never mind. How about the army? Have the men been paid?

JAILER: Nobody's been paid for two months.

LUMUMBA: Hmm. Maybe it's because there's no money left in the till. And what about Mokutu? And Kala? And the UN? What have they been doing?

SOLDIER: That's what I'd like to know. If the treasury's empty, where's the money? Just tell me that. You ought to know, you were a minister. But hell, you're like all the rest of them, a nigger egghead.

LUMUMBA: Take it easy, friend. Take it easy. You want to know where the money is. I'll tell you. It's in Katanga. Yes, sir, in Katanga. In Tzumbi's treasury. And I'll tell you something else. It's because I tried to get it back that I'm here!

SOLDIER: That's the truth. That's what I've been telling the boys. Some believe me, some don't. Anyway, it's a mess. You say it's the Katanga police that get the money?

LUMUMBA: Sure, the police. And Tzumbi. And Msiri. And the Belgians. But come along, men, why all these gloomy thoughts? Let's have another round.

The SOLDIERS *pour themselves beer. Glasses are passed around.*

LUMUMBA: Soldiers, I see that a lot of you are Batetelas.

Glad to know it. I'm a Mutetela myself. We're the tribe that put up the last fight against the Belgians sixty years ago. We saved the honor of the whole Congo. And I'm doing my duty as a Mutetela by fighting the last battle maybe, to prevent our country from falling into the clutches of a new colonialism.

Soldiers of other tribes, I trust you no less; I know the army as a whole is loyal to me as its legitimate commander. The army had nothing to do with Mokutu's treachery. His tools were his hand-picked praetorians, his paratroopers. He puts them up at the Hotel Memling and stuffs them like geese. Where does he get the money? I'll tell you. Partly from the Americans. But mostly out of the funds the UN gave him to pay you with. You fellows aren't staying at the Memling. I know the life you lead. You do all the dirty work. No hope of promotion, no pay. Your ribs stick out so the top brass and their body-guards can roll in fat. When I appointed the first black officers, how could I imagine that quicker than lava spurts from a volcano, a new caste would be born, the caste of colonels and new masters, and that those voracious, insatiable dogs would monopolize all the benefits of Congolese freedom.

SOLDIER: To hell with Mokutu. We're letting you out. Go on home. Maybe you'll help us fill our bellies.

SECOND SOLDIER: Hurray for Lumumba! When he talks, he says something.

SOLDIERS: Down with Mokutu! Down with Mokutu!

SOLDIER: If I catch him, I'll cut his gizzard out.

LUMUMBA: I respect your opinions and I don't want to influence you. But I want you all to know that the situation is critical. Two months after independence

the kid is walking into the gullet of a wild beast. If
I, Lumumba, brace myself and hold on for dear life,
it's to save the Congo from the claws of the beast.
Will you help me?

SOLDIERS *(shouting)*: We're with you. You're our chief.
Down with Mokutu!

The SOLDIERS *open the gates of the prison and carry*
LUMUMBA *out in triumph.*

Scene 2

African bar. Men and women. Same atmosphere as in Act I, Scene 2. A woman sings.

WOMAN:

> Who's seen my husband?
> Nobody's seen him.
> A bamboo splinter
> Has pierced my heart.

Suddenly the door opens. Enter LUMUMBA, MPOLO, *and* OKITO.

MAMA MAKOSI: Patrice! You here?

LUMUMBA: See for yourself.

MAMA MAKOSI: I knew they couldn't hold you.

LUMUMBA: It's a good thing to have faith. A lot of people wouldn't have given two cents for Lumumba's hide. Yes, here I am. Free. Freed by our Congolese soldiers. Go get my wife and children. This is my headquarters from now on.

MAMA MAKOSI: You're right. They betrayed you, the whole lot of them. Kala. Mokutu. Your buddy Mokutu. I never did like him. He looks like a sneaky little girl. Here you're safe, the house is yours, and the people will protect you.

83

LUMUMBA: You'll have to forgive me. My presence is likely to upset your routine around here.

MAMA MAKOSI: Never mind about that. Just tell us what those scoundrels did to you.

WOMEN: Yes, yes, tell us about it.

The SANZA PLAYER *sings.*

> Nut, nut
> One cocoanut, just one,
> Its oil is enough
> To fill the bowl.

LUMUMBA: Thank you, friend. You've given me the courage and strength to defy the whole world. But what do you want me to tell you? The details? What's the good of details? I've better things to tell you. I'll tell you about Africa. Yes, Africa! The eyes, the back, the flanks! Africa is like a man who wakes up in the morning and sees that he's being attacked on all sides.

Attacked by hawks and vultures. He hasn't hid from one before the next is on him with its dripping beak. Makes me think of our Mukongo dance of the twelve masks: we had riches, beauty, assurance, potent medicines, and then came the Spirit of Jealousy and Evil with its powerful fetishes, sullying the cheeks of our virgins, felling our warriors, bringing corruption and dissension. A hideous nightmare! In the end, thank God, the Spirit of Evil was defeated, and we brought back Prosperity. Do you hear me, all of you? We'll bring back Prosperity, and we'll keep her. Prosperity's coming back to the Congo, friends. Let's drink to her! But let's not be selfish. I'm going to pass on the good news to our foreign friends, to the whole world. Call in the gentlemen of the press.

MAN: Yes, the press. Let them come. But we want them to

know that you're our king! Our legitimate king! Put
on the leopard skin.

CROWD: Yes! Yes! The leopard skin!

LUMUMBA: Friends, don't make me do that. One day in the
bush I met my animal soul: it had the form of a bird.
My sign is a bird, that's better than a leopard. To enter the new day, the bronze wings of the ibis.

MAN: You're right. The chiefs and kings have all betrayed
us. You're better than they are. You are our inspired
guide, our Messiah. Glory be, Simon Kibangu is back
again.

CROWD (*singing*):

> We are the orphan children.
> Dark is the night, hard is the way.
> Almighty God, who's going to help us?
> Father Congo, who's going to give us a hand?

The MAN *holds out to* LUMUMBA *a kind of stole which*
LUMUMBA *waves away.*

LUMUMBA: And what do I do but give you a hand? With all
my strength. Beyond my strength. But I won't wear a
stole any more than a leopard skin. It may come as a
disappointment to you, but I'm not Simon Kibangu. He
wanted to give you back your strength, our Congo
ngolo, and for that he deserves to be remembered. He
wanted to go see God all alone, all alone, as your ambassador, to demand your rights, and for that you have
every reason to glorify him. The white men confiscated
God for their own benefit, and Simon Kibangu tried
to win him back. But they robbed us of more than
God, they robbed Africa of herself. Africa is hungry
for its own being. And that's why I don't want to be
a Messiah or a prophet. My only weapon is my tongue;

I speak, I awaken, I'm not a redresser of wrongs. I don't perform miracles, I'm a redresser of life. I speak, I give Africa back to herself. I speak, and I give Africa to the world.

Uncertainty in the crowd. Enter PAULINE LUMUMBA. *She and* LUMUMBA *embrace.*

PAULINE: Oh God, how happy I am! I was so worried. Those people are brutes. They're capable of anything. But here you are! Saved! But you're not safe here in Leo. We're going away. To Stanleyville. I've arranged everything. In Stanleyville the whole population's behind you.

LUMUMBA: Stanleyville? All I've been doing is fighting secession, and you want me to organize a new secession? No, I won't desert, I won't run away. And there's nothing to be afraid of here. My enemies have learned their lesson. They know the Congo can't get along without me.

PAULINE: You've always been stubborn and intractable. A regular mule. Does that man even give me a thought? Patrice, I'm talking to you. And you look up above me.

LUMUMBA: Above, below, I don't know. Both, I guess. Above I see Africa, and below, mingled with the muffled drum of my blood, the Congo.

PAULINE: Admit, Patrice, that I never turned you aside from your duty, but Africa's not your wife. You have other responsibilities besides the weal and woe of Africa. Do you remember the day we were married, Patrice? My father poured the palm wine, you took a sip, you held out the glass for me, I took a sip, and so we drank together till the glass was empty. I haven't got the name of a country or a river, I've got the name of a woman: Pauline. That's all I have to say. Except one question: Do you want the people to see me with my head shaved, following a funeral procession? And the children? Do you want them to be orphans?

LUMUMBA: It can't be helped. In my heart I've always called you Pauline Congo, and your double name has helped me doubly to control my weakness. And I'm prepared to defy the whole world if I know I can count on you. If I die, I leave the children the legacy of a great struggle. And you will help them, guide them, arm them. But let's not be pessimistic. I'm going to live through this struggle and win. Forgive me, Pauline. Go to Brazzaville, try to see Luis. Tell him what's been happening. And now I have to speak to the press.

PAULINE (*exits slowly, singing*):

> Alas, alas, who's seen my husband?
> Nobody's seen my husband.
> A bamboo splinter
> Has pierced my heart.

Enter the gentlemen of the press.

LUMUMBA: Make yourselves as comfortable as you can, gentlemen. Excuse the surroundings. They don't mean a thing. No, as a matter of fact, they mean a great deal. They mean that I put my trust in the people. It's a humble place, but here at least the heart of the Congo beats in its own way, more freely than in any government palace. I've called you here to tell you, and for you to tell the world, that the Congo is taking up where it left off. I was deposed by a childish coup d'état, but now I'm back in the saddle. My government is the only legal government of the Congo. It intends to make itself respected, to restore and reinforce the unity of the Congo. We do not seek revenge. The era of hatred is ended. Now it is time to build the Republic in peace and dignity. Gentlemen, I am counting on you to inform world public opinion of our peaceful intentions. My government will do everything in its power to maintain friendly relations with all foreign countries. In return, I expect every foreign government to recognize that the Congo is an independent country and intends to preserve its full independence and sovereignty.

REPORTER: Mr. Lumumba, that sounds like a prime minister's speech of investiture. But aren't you being unrealistic? Are you aware of the present political situation? Are you aware of your own situation?

LUMUMBA: Thank you for your concern. Let me set your mind at rest. I am the Prime Minister of the Republic of the Congo. I have the support of the people, and the Parliament has given me an overwhelming vote of confidence. I therefore have every legitimate right to speak in the name of the Congo. Gentlemen of the press, it is your noble mission to inform your readers. I call upon you to do so with scrupulous honesty.

Women rush in, in a panic.

MAMA MAKOSI: Patrice, the paratroopers! They've surrounded the house.

MPOLO: Don't worry about them, Patrice, our boys are ready. The people are with us. Mokutu's thugs will get more than they bargained for.

LUMUMBA: No, Mpolo. There has been enough bloodshed.

MPOLO: But we can't just sit here with our hands folded.

LUMUMBA: I'm not a religious man, but I am convinced of this: that justice cannot be won by violence.

MPOLO: In this situation non-violence is suicide.

LUMUMBA: Exactly, Mpolo. If I have to die, I want to die like Gandhi. All right, show those people in. I grant them an audience.

Enter KALA, MOKUTU, *and a group of* PARATROOPERS.

MOKUTU (*to the* PARATROOPERS) : Get rid of all these people. (*To the newspapermen.*) Excuse me, gentlemen, the show is over. Now we have work to do. I'll see you again in due time. Good-bye.

The newspapermen, girls, and customers are removed.

KALA (*to* LUMUMBA) : I come to you with an offer. It may seem surprising. But not if you bear in mind that for me the welfare of my country outweighs all other considerations. I hope I find you in the same frame of mind.

LUMUMBA: I have never served any other interests than those of the Congo. Say your piece.

KALA: Our government cannot function without an executive.

LUMUMBA: I'm glad to hear you say that. I am the prime minister. I have not been overthrown by the Parliament. Consequently there is no government crisis. If there seems to be, it is only because certain people have acted illegally.

KALA: You don't seem to understand. No one can turn back the clock. Try to be realistic for once. Ileo is the man of the situation. He is level-headed, reassuring. The country is in flames. Let him put out the fire. Once that's done, we shall see . . . I'm only asking you to have a little patience. Just a little patience. The banana ripens slowly.

LUMUMBA: I hate time. I detest your *slowly*. And why do you always want to reassure people? Give me a man who upsets them, who tells them what the bad shepherds are doing to us.

KALA: I am offering you a place in the Cabinet. Choose any portfolio you wish. Vice-president, minister of state, minister of anything you like. Do you or do you not accept?

LUMUMBA (*airily*): Say, that reminds me, how's Youlou getting along? Yes, Fulbert Youlou. I hear he's sent away to Paris for a new soutane. Pure nylon.

KALA (*shocked*): This is no time for jokes. I expect a serious answer.

LUMUMBA: It's not a bad idea, come to think of it. Gives his wives less washing to do. But don't get hot and bothered. I'll give you your serious answer. Mr. President, I will not be your Quisling.

KALA: What's that?

LUMUMBA: I will not, by my presence, lend support to a policy that I disavow. And still less will I sponsor a government of corrupt traitors.

KALA: Do you know what I came here for? To save your life. To give you a chance to save your skin. Don't tempt fate.

LUMUMBA: Do you know what you're asking of me?

KALA: Asking? Are you so sure that you're in a position to give?

LUMUMBA: If I weren't, you wouldn't have honored me with your visit. You came here to ask me for the seal of legitimacy. Very well, in the name of the Congo, I refuse it.

MOKUTU: Mr. President, there's no use arguing. You're talking to a lunatic. Never mind. I'll take him down a peg.

KALA: You asked for it, Patrice. Good-bye. He's all yours, Mokutu.

MOKUTU: All right, Mr. Lumumba, it's your funeral, you ordered it. Soldiers. This man is your prisoner.

Scene 3

Elisabethville, the seat of the Katanga government. The dominant characteristics of the Katangese leaders are hypocrisy and ecclesiastical unctuousness, except for MSIRI, *who is a savage.* ZIMBWÉ *and* TRAVÉLÉ *are slightly drunk. During the whole scene whiskey and champagne are poured generously.*

MOKUTU: It is not a pleasant mission that has brought me here. You have violated your agreement with the Leopoldville government which I represent. You stated your conditions. They were reasonable and we subscribed to them. We have carried out our side of the bargain. And you? Katanga has not only maintained its secession but given the whole world to understand . . .

TZUMBI: Come, come . . . An agreement. That's a big word. There has been no agreement . . . in the strict sense. Just friendly conversations among good friends . . .

ZIMBWÉ: Tut, tut. Words. Let's not talk about words. Agreement, treaty, conversation. What difference does it make? The main thing, in my opinion, is to distinguish between the spirit and the letter. For the letter kills . . .

TRAVÉLÉ: You took the words out of my mouth. And the spirit saves. (*He laughs idiotically.*)

TZUMBI: Zimbwé and Travélé are right. The spirit of our
conversations was that the elimination of Lumumba
was the *sine qua non* . . .

MOKUTU: Good Lord, man. Haven't we eliminated him?

MSIRI: Don't be childish. Do we have to spell it out for
you? A single blow isn't fatal to a snake like Lumumba.
Lumumba is still a menace to Congo.

TZUMBI: Forgive our good friend Msiri, he may be uncouth
but he has a heart of gold. And plenty of wisdom. It's
true that we don't care much for Leopoldville. The
UN, your populace, your soldiery . . . Too much noise
and agitation. And I don't want to be unkind, but you
people in the government lead the life of Reilly . . .
Oh well, that's none of my business. The point is we
think Lumumba would be better off in Katanga.

MOKUTU: He's a troublesome prisoner. I'd be only too
glad to get rid of him. But sending him to Katanga
would raise certain delicate problems—both domestic
and international. The people are devoted to Lumumba. And you know how world opinion feels about
democratic forms, what a fetish they make of democracy.

ZIMBWÉ: Tut tut. Democracy. That's a big word with you
Leopoldville people. Well, my dear colleague, we're
democrats too, here in Katanga, but in our opinion,
democracy means only one thing: democracy is what
serves the interests of the people. And this transfer,
I am sure we all agree, will serve the interests of this
country's people.

TRAVÉLÉ (*laughing*): Just as I said. It's the spirit that saves.
The spirit.

MSIRI: You spoke just now of an internal problem. There's

no internal problem. The people! The people! Bah! The people obey the man with the biggest stick. If you know how to command, the rabble will crawl. That's the only question. Do you know how to command? Will you ever learn to be chiefs?

MOKUTU: All right, all right, Msiri, don't get excited, we'll try. In any case I will submit your proposal to the government. Good-bye.

TZUMBI: Au revoir. You mean au revoir. Because this time we can call it an agreement. We are bound by an agreement. Remember that. And don't forget to tell Kala that this time we'll let Lumumba land. (*He laughs.*)

ZIMBWÉ: Land. Hee-hee. I get it.

TRAVÉLÉ (*laughing*): It's the spirit that saves . . . and the letter that kills . . . And when I say kill, I mean kill. Your health, Mokutu!

As the light fades, the SANZA PLAYER *passes, singing.*

> Oh little sparrow hawk, oh! oh!
> Oh little sparrow hawk, spread your wings.
> The sun's drinking blood, oh oh!
> Little sparrow hawk, little sparrow hawk,
> What blood is the sun drinking?

Scene 4

United Nations Headquarters in New York.

HAMMARSKJÖLD: Have you heard the news? I've received a cable. They've taken Lumumba to Katanga; there's good reason to fear for his life . . . it's dreadful.

MATTHEW CORDELIER: Yes, in view of the customs of that delightful country, the Lumumba question seems to be settled once and for all.

HAMMARSKJÖLD: It doesn't seem to trouble you very much.

CORDELIER: Since Mr. Lumumba is not a personal friend of mine, I can only take a professional view of the matter. You will admit that it simplifies the political situation of the Congo.

HAMMARSKJÖLD: Tell the truth, Cordelier. You hated him. Why not admit it? And you people call yourselves neutrals. I should have kept my eyes open. You never stopped plotting against him.

CORDELIER: The UN is an organization, no, an organism that doesn't take kindly to the foreign body known as sentimentality.

HAMMARSKJÖLD: I have a strong case against you. You kept him out of the radio station, you prevented him from defending himself when his enemies had every opportunity to spread their insidious propaganda. On pretext of reserving the Leopoldville air field for United Nations planes, you cut him off from the outside world while Belgian planes were landing in Katanga around the clock ... In short, we pinned down his arms while his enemies struck him. Nice work!

CORDELIER: Your sympathies are carrying you away. You sound like the Soviet delegate.

HAMMARSKJÖLD: The worst part of it is that Zorine is right, thanks to you. You deceived me. The whole lot of you. And to think that I lent my name to your odious acts.

CORDELIER: Mr. Secretary General, let me defend myself.

HAMMARSKJÖLD: No, you can't expect me to say what Lord Jim said to Doramin: "I take it all on myself." No, I won't be silent. I've been silent long enough. Tell me, Cordelier, what do you think of Jesus Christ?

CORDELIER: That's an odd question. I'm a Christian ... a Methodist, and you know it.

HAMMARSKJÖLD: What do I care if you're a Methodist and a Christian? Anybody can beat his breast and say "I'm a Christian" ... What I'm asking you is not what Matthew Cordelier thinks of Christ—who cares?—but what side you, Matthew Cordelier, would have been on one thousand nine hundred and sixty-one years ago when in Judaea, under the Roman occupation, one of your contemporaries, a certain Jesus, was arrested and put to death. And now get out of here, you murderer of Christ!

Scene 5

A training camp in Katanga. A white MERCENARY, *in front of him a dummy representing a Negro. He cleans his revolver and sings.*

MERCENARY:

> In the south, in the tropics,
> in the desert, in the jungle,
> in the marshes of the deltas
>
> rain, mosquitoes, fever
> weather-beaten skin
> knight of the new day
> my heart swells in my breast
> for liberty and justice.

(*He stands up, goes into position, and fires at the dummy.*) Swine, baboon, savage, magician, ungrateful bastard! Nun raper. Bing! Bing! Bing! (*He fires.*) Ah, the devils! They won't die. Look at him with his big white eyes and his big red face. Bing, bing, bing! Take that! (*He fires.*) I've seen them. Even when they're dead, they keep coming at you. We had to kill them ten times. They say their magicians promise to turn our bullets into water. Bing! Bing! Bing! (*He fires, the dummy topples over.*) I don't guess that one turned into water. (*He laughs.*) But Christ, I'm wringing wet!

Oof! It's hot. Christ, am I thirsty! Stinking country!
(*He wipes his forehead and pours himself a drink. He
sings.*)

> I had some trouble with my folks,
> They didn't like my kind of jokes,
> The fights, the debts, the broads, the junk,
> I wasn't cut out for a monk.
> My girl was cute, my girl had curves,
> But she was getting on my nerves.
> I hugged her tight, I packed my trunk,
> And lit out for the Congo.

It grows dark. When the light goes on again, the white
MERCENARY *is still holding his smoking revolver, but
on the ground the dummy has been replaced by two
corpses,* OKITO *and* MPOLO. *Enter* MSIRI *and a mercenary, pushing* LUMUMBA. *Suddenly* MSIRI *flings himself on* LUMUMBA *and strikes him in the face.*

MSIRI: D'you see the way your buddies spat out the
bullets? Ha ha ha. Well, that leaves just you and me.
(*The* MERCENARY *tries to interfere.* MSIRI *snatches his
bayonet.*) No, I've got a personal account to settle
with our friend here. (*To* LUMUMBA.) I'm told you
think you're invulnerable. Is that a fact? Will you
answer when you're spoken to?

LUMUMBA: It's Msiri all right. I was expecting this meeting. It had to be. We are the two opposing forces.
You're the invention of the past. And I an inventor
of the future.

MSIRI: They tell me you Kasai people have powerful
magic. Ocelot skin or some such thing. This is the
time to show what it's worth.

LUMUMBA: My magic is an invulnerable idea. As invincible

as a people's hope, as the fire that spreads from bush to bush, as the pollen in the wind, as a root in the blind earth.

MSIRI (*prodding him with the bayonet*): How about this? Or this? I suppose you don't feel it? Cutting into your hide ... cutting, cutting ... closer and closer to the heart!

LUMUMBA: Careful. My heart has a hard pit, a flint that will break your blade. It's the honor of Africa.

MSIRI (*sneering*): Africa! Africa doesn't give a hoot in hell. Africa can't do a thing for you. Msiri is right here. And Msiri is man enough to drink your blood and eat your heart.

LUMUMBA: All night I heard wailing and laughing, sighing and scolding ... that was the hyena!

MSIRI: You arrogant son-of-a-bitch! Can't you see death looking you in the eye? You're living your death and you don't even notice it.

LUMUMBA: I'm dying my life, and that's good enough for me.

MSIRI: Look! (*He thrusts in the blade.*) All right, prophet, what do you see now?

LUMUMBA:

> I will be field, I will be pasture,
> I will be with the Wagenia fisherman
> I will be with the Kivu drover
> I will be on the mountain, I will be in the ravine.

MSIRI: Let's get this over with. (*He presses the bayonet.*)

LUMUMBA: Oh, the dew over Africa. Comrades, I see the flaming tree, I see Pygmies with axes busy around the precarious trunk, but the head grows, the head grows, and it calls out to the tumbling sky in the first foam of dawn.

MSIRI: Bastard! (LUMUMBA *falls.*) (*To the* MERCENARY.) Dog, finish him off.

A shot. The MERCENARY *gives* LUMUMBA *the coup de grâce. Darkness. When the light goes on, a group of statuelike figures is seen in the background: the* BANKERS, KALA, TZUMBI, MOKUTU. *Slightly to one side,* HAMMARSKJÖLD. PAULINE LUMUMBA *enters.*

PAULINE:

A cage, four clouds. Lycaon, Lycaon
        of the flashing eyes!
The alphabet of fear
Mumbled as the buzzards fly overhead.
Close to the ground treason nibbles its shadow.
Higher, a hovering batlike flight of premonitions.
Below, on the black-white that torpor
Pours unceasingly, shipwreck
Repeats with gentle beckonings its invitation
To the most beautiful marriage of disaster and the
        stars.

Giggling slightly, the SANZA PLAYER *steps forward, dressed like a Congolese sorcerer; straw skirt, bells on his wrists and ankles. He crosses the stage chanting.*

SANZA PLAYER:

Hey you, the great god Nzambi,
What a big fool you are!
You eat our ribs, you eat our asses,
Hey, Nzambi, what a big fool you are!
You eat our hearts and livers!
Hey, Nzambi. You eat too much.

About to leave the stage, he turns back, faces the audience and twirls his mpiya, *a bundle of cock plumes, an instrument of divination.*

> Sing, women! Men, give me song!
> In the sand of falsehood I scratch.
> Spur, I scratch! Down to the truth I scratch.
>> Scratching spur!
> I am the *nganga,*
>> The cock of divination.

HAMMARSKJÖLD: Congo!
Through the matrix of original sin
The logic of things past penetrates
To the black hearth of our selves,
The terrible inner fire that gives forth evil.
Oh, that the just should become unjust;
That sincerity should become a machine to crush
     sincerity!
Oh God, why did they choose me
To preside over their diabolical alchemy!
But Thy will be done! Thy will, not mine.
I await the order. I hear the order.
It's only the first step that's hard.

He takes a step.

It's only the first step that counts.

He goes out.

A BANKER: For my part, I see no ground for political speculation. A mere episode of folklore, as it were, an outcropping of that Bantu mentality which periodically, even in the best of them, bursts through the frail varnish of civilization.

   In any case, and this is my main point, you've

seen for yourselves that we had nothing to do with it. Nothing whatever. (*He goes out with great dignity.*)

TZUMBI (*stepping forward*): You'll see. You'll see. I'll be blamed for the whole business. I tell you in all sincerity: this crime is part of a plot against my person. (*He goes out.*)

KALA: See for yourself: nobody obeys me in the Congo. I told them to prune the tree, not to pull it up by the roots. (*He goes out.*)

MOKUTU: I had no personal animosity toward him. Everyone knew that, that's why the politicians of this country were so careful not to inform me of the plot against him. Oh yes, I know. I found it necessary to put a temporary stop to his career, to neutralize him, as I put it. And that will be held against me. But God himself has an eraser on his pencil. I fully expected that what political expediency had made me do, political expediency would make me undo. But crime foiled my plans.

Darkness, then light.
A sign indicates: July, 1966.
A public square in Kinshasa, Independence Day.

WOMAN: Hurrah for Mokutu. Mokutu uhuru!

MAMA MAKOSI: Uhuru Lumumba!

WOMAN: Careful, citizen. Uhuru Mokutu is what you've got to say.

MAMA MAKOSI: I say what I think. Uhuru Lumumba.

THE WOMAN: In any case, down with colonialism! Boo! Boo! Here come the coffins!

MAMA MAKOSI: The coffins? What coffins?

SANZA PLAYER: Death butts into everything in the Congo!

WOMAN: Why not? Death is life. The first coffin is for the Belgian Congo; the second is for daddy's Congo; the third is for tribal conflict. It's wonderful! Hurrah for Mokutu!

A VOICE: Hush! Hush. The General is going to speak!

A VOICE: Shut up. We want to listen.

MOKUTU (*in a leopard skin, haranguing the crowd*):
Patrice, martyr, athlete, hero—I turn to you for the strength to carry on my task. (*Sensation.* MOKUTU *pauses for a moment with head bowed.*)

Congolese,
It is my wish that from this day on
The finest of our boulevards should bear his name;
That the place where he was struck down become the
        shrine of our nation;
and that a statue erected at the gate of what was
        formerly Leopoldville
signify to the world
that the piety of a nation will never cease
to make reparation for our crime,
the crime of which we are all guilty.
Congolese, may this day be the beginning of a new
        era for the Congo!

As the curtain slowly falls, the SANZA PLAYER *steps forward and sings:*

The sorgho grows
The bird rises from the ground
Why shouldn't man
Have a right to change?

If a man is hungry
Do you deny him food?

So why say no to a country
That's thirsting for hope.

But just a minute! Let's not go off half-cocked.
A beginning is only a beginning
And if we're going to do this thing
Let's not do it by halves.

If you're going to grow
Then grow straight
And if you're going to rise from the ground
Then you must learn to soar.

Everyone's got a nose.
It grows, it shows, it blows.
Now that you're standing on feet of your own
Getting stronger and fatter
You'd better keep it clean.
This is the end of my chatter.

THE END